NEW HORIZONS IN FLOWER ARRANGEMENT

New
Horizons
in
Flower
Arrangement

By MYRA J. BROOKS *with* MARY ALICE *and* JOHN P. ROCHE

M. BARROWS AND COMPANY INC.

NEW YORK

TO ALL CRAFTSMEN

who create not alone with the intellect,

but with the hand and the heart as well.

Foreword

A new book of flower arrangement usually resides on my bedside table where I can dip into it briefly before going to sleep. I started to glance through the manuscript of this one and couldn't put it down. Besides the visual pleasure of the compositions, an obbligato of human experience hums through the text and echoes in the creative use of plant material linked in design and association with articles fashioned by other hands. Besides seeing beauty in these objects, the authors were interested as well in the people who made them. Their quest led the authors on many trails to many doors and to deep convictions. They found the initiative, inventiveness, and self-reliance of the craftsman a warm and lilting song above the monotone of mechanization, stereotype, and conformity too often accepted as standard in today's world. Their creative handwork set the key for the authors' compositions.

The objects of their inspiration range widely. To recall a few—wood-carved gulls from Maine, a page of Japanese calligraphy, a shepherd's flute from Israel, a blue bird made of bits of sparkling glass, the gauzy texture of hand-loomed drapery, a rug, a screen, a table. The voices that are heard besides the authors' are not necessarily big voices in the art world, not bold Picassos who revolutionize the art of a day or age. These are of people who fashion something of beauty from material at hand and out of their own experience. Their satisfaction is from the doing, not so much from thinking of their claim to immortality or their position in history or art.

It is soon observed from the photographic illustrations that the crafted objects are not used merely as accessories to the floral arrangements. One complements the other in compositions which are fresh and often daring in the relationships of objects, plant material, space, and balance of the designs. The concept may be small and exquisite as a jewel in a setting, subtle as a shadow, or large as a whole room. The mood may be reverent, whimsical, or gay. The plant material may be a simple rhythmic spray, a grouping of plant forms, or a highly stylized arrangement of flowers. Each composition expresses some phase of a larger meaning the authors have found: the interdependence of man's work and the beauty of nature.

I have known the authors for many years and have been cognizant of the development of their skills and their philosophy. Each is now such a master of his medium that they can portray exactly what they intend. It is no wonder that the Roches have won prizes for their flower photography, including a medal of the Royal Horticultural Society of London, and that their book, *Photographing Your Flowers* is a standard guide. In the present book the Roches use light and shade and color as a maestro uses his knowledge to interpret great music.

Myra Brooks is no less skilled in flower arrangement and she has won so many awards in competition that it must be possible for her to have a room papered with blue ribbons. Her three *Workbooks of Flower Arrangement* are widely used in teaching. That she grows much of the plant material she uses influences her treatment of it: she never imposes upon a plant a posture or performance inconsistent with its nature.

In the previous book in which these authors collaborated, *The Magic World of Flower Arranging*, they drew their inspiration principally from things of nature — rocks, shells, the sea, the pond, the harvest. In *New Horizons* they have reached out to include the imaginative work of man. This concern with other human beings is not surprising when you know that Mrs. Brooks has worked for 15 years in gardening therapy and, since 1949, with psychiatric patients of Lyons Veterans Hospital, as a volunteer member of the Green Thumb Corps of the Garden Club of New Jersey.

The results of these years of experience, of developing technical skills and a personal philosophy, show forth in this beautiful book, truly leading the reader to new horizons in "the joy of living, the joy of seeing and the joy of doing."

HELEN S. HULL

CONTENTS

9

Acknowledgments

ONE of the greatest pleasures in preparing this book has been our association with the many remarkable people who have helped us so greatly with their ideas and their possessions as well as with their interest and enthusiasm.

Thanks are due to the Westfield Flower Shop for their co-operation; to Mr. and Mrs. Dennis Lever—and all our other good friends in Florida—who helped us gather our tropical material; Mr. and Mrs. Russell H. Jones, Jr. for the material from California and Oregon; and to all those who loaned us their treasures: Mrs. Mary Coates for her Indian baskets and Turkish robe; Mrs. Eric Feasey for the ivory from her collection; Mrs. Raymond Foulkrod for her Nantucket basket; Maxwell's Antique Shop for the ruby lustres; and, most of all, Mr. and Mrs. Edward Candor and Mrs. Everett Rowley who were always able to provide from their fine collections just the things we needed.

There is an extra, heartfelt thank you for Mrs. Rowley, for her generosity with an extraordinary store of garden materials both fresh and dried, her meticulous needlework, and her untiring efforts to track down desired facts and artifacts.

Our gratitude goes to the Edward Candors, the C. J. Owens, and the Pete Carrs for allowing us to take photographs in their homes; to the various artists who allowed us to use their attractive shops as settings for flower-and-craft compositions; Elizabeth Kaufman, Wendell Gilley, Ruth and Denis Vibert, Stell and Shevis, and Martin Stan Buchner; and to the members of the staff of the Newark Museum—Miss Eleanor Olson, Mrs. Charles Miller, Mr. Edward Chandless, and Mr. Hunter Ross—who could not have been more helpful.

We appreciate the courtesy of Mr. Charles Lee Burwell of the American Craftsmen's Council who furnished us with background information regarding the present crafts movement; and of the potter Denis Vibert, the violin-maker Alvah M. Batchelder, the flutists, Ziphion Azta and Yeshiva Safari, and the flower-show workers the Misses Florence and Harriet Hopping, who allowed us to photograph them. To them, and to all of the craftsmen who gave so generously of their time in telling us of their work and explaining the philosophy behind it, we offer our sincere thanks.

Introduction

THE art of flower arrangement in this country has had comparatively few years to develop; progress has been made by utilizing the established traditions of other lands and periods. However, there has not been time enough — nor the artistic climate — for a gradual, unself-conscious evolution of a deeply rooted tradition of our own. Today, flower arrangement, along with the other "civilized" arts, is consciously striving for "individual" artistic expression.

Individuality, as the word tells us, means undividedness, that in which all elements are fused into a unity. A work in which such unity has been achieved is naturally set apart from others in which it has not. In today's world many artists tend toward disintegration rather than integration, discarding the traditional use of intellect plus a disciplined hand and an understanding heart in favor of a dehumanized art arising solely from the intellect, or of a private, therapeutic art arising solely from emotion. They thus fragment their powers rather than unify them and so reject true individuality. In order to set their work apart they rely on originality at all costs, and this is what individuality has come to mean to them.

The current drive for sensational originality has cut art off from its historic traditions, depriving the young artist of a firm foothold from which to take his bearing, depriving the artist who works within the tradition of the needed encouragement toward natural growth, and depriving mankind of that continuity in the language of art which is essential to its function as a means of communication.

If flower arrangement follows this course, it will end as another private art without the power to evoke a wide response. In any case, the detachment of flower arrangement from the world of nature, to become either an intellectual exercise in design or the non-communicable expression of personal emotion, is an obvious reversal of terms and intent.

Insistence that we look upon a stalk of grass purely as a collection of lines and curves would be to cut ourselves off from the half of experience that tells us this grass — like any growing plant — is a symbol of the continual re-creation of life on earth. It is equally true that insistence on pure symbolism is sentimental rather than artistic, and that the refusal to observe and use the physical elements of the design cuts us off from the other half of experience.

This does not mean that these qualities are equally present within every subject, or that a subject lacking in one or the other cannot give pleasure. For example, iron scrollwork without particular association can be enjoyed as pure design, although a deeper satisfaction comes from a carved angel where the outward appearance is fused with the inner meaning. Plant compositions made for such pieces naturally reflect their character. Each type has its place, but this should not affect our realization of their respective values.

We agree with Aldous Huxley that "the greatest work of art is that which unifies into one harmonious whole the greatest number and most diverse elements of human experience." We remember the work of Inbal, the dance theater of Israel, and know that its deeply moving power and beauty was the result of such unification, the harmonious integration of music, dance, song, history, religious faith, and feeling for the land -- work based upon ancient traditions, transmitted through the creative mind.

Inbal is a communal effort and as such quite different from flower arrangement. But we do have one important thing in common — our creations exist for a short time only, affording an opportunity for continual re-creation and a frequency of execution which should result in an ever-growing understanding of purpose and meaning.

Yet this impermanence of flower arrangement has in part kept it from being considered an art in the West. Only in the East, where the impermanence of nature is understood to be the basis for life — where art and nature are one — has flower arrangement reached the status of great art which truly illumines human experience. Whether it will ever be so understood in the West seems doubtful as our scientific, mechanized society grows farther and farther from nature.

We are not proposing that the arrangements in this book are great art, but we do hope that our readers will find here something to give them pleasure, to encourage and to challenge them to experience at first hand the beauties of the natural world and the gratification of using its materials to create imaginative designs of more than superficial interest.

Imagination is the recognition of relationships among all the elements of experience, the perception of outward form as a symbol of inner meaning. Naturally, the wider the understanding of any one mind, through continual exploration of varied viewpoints and aspects of life, the greater the creativeness of the imagination.

This book started from some casual visits to craft shops where we found original objects which were most compatible with our art-craft of flower arrangement. As our interest deepened, we discover many designer-craftsmen whose feeling for line, form, texture, and color reflected an awareness of these same qualities in nature. We did not seek the most costly works signed by the most famous names; among those pieces available to any interested person we found much which stimulated our imagination and complimented the plant material with which we worked.

Our contacts with the artist-craftsmen before and during the writing of this book have immeasurably enriched our understanding, giving us new insight into the present state of art in our society, into the work and philosophy of the craftsmen, and into our own also.

The one thing of which we have become most firmly convinced is the need for a tradition, not a tradition which is obsessed with the past but one which builds on the past a sustaining vision of the future, one in which a humanized language of art will contain both design interest and imaginative content expressed through fine material and fine workmanship.

Here is a great part of our bond with craftsmen who are making things to be used. They know that there must be fine materials and fine workmanship in their products if these are to fulfill their functional purpose. When Alvah Batchelder says that a violin is no better than the wood that goes into it, that the workmanship makes the difference between a violin that will make real music and one that will not, the point is easily understood. He knows the value of fine materials and the respect they merit.

The materials of flower arrangement are the most beautiful and varied of all, being drawn from the whole world of nature. The fragility and impermanence of most of them demand a spontaneity of arrangement, but a spontaneity based on complete mastery of technique. And they should not be treated as lifeless, "pure" art forms.

Recognition of design in nature should not be divided from recognition of its function and association. Only when all its facets are realized can we feel its true beauty.

An important purpose of flower arranging is to make possible the enjoyment of nature within the home in the most artistically satisfying way. When so used it becomes even more closely allied to the work of craftsmen, which also increases the distinction and warmth of a home with the special qualities of handwork made from the materials of nature.

Another bond with the craftsman is our mutual belief that, in the words of the potter Denis Vibert, we must "affirm the ideal of a man working for the sake of the work itself. . . . There should be joy in the making of things as well as in the using." There is a particular joy in the work of the flower arranger, especially when she grows her own material, following the pattern of the seasons, watching the day-by-day variations in color, form, and habit of growth. This is in addition to the joy found in the actual work of gardening, and, later, in using the materials she has grown to create flower compositions.

The potter Bernard Leach says, "The whole world stands in need of a fresh understanding of work as an expression of the spirit of man. . . . The ideal, whether for man himself, or for the work of his hands, is oneness, or attunement . . . between the beauty in man's work and beauty in nature. . . . There is no room for overstressed individualism. We have not only split the atom, but ourselves to boot, and somehow we have to put the bits, heart, head, and hand, together again."

This is a restatement of a very old tradition which has gone out of fashion. We would like to see it return to fashion and become the new tradition for all the arts — and most particularly for the art of flower arrangement.

PART I

Flower Arrangers' Holidays

Handcraft Trails and Roadside Flowers

IT was a real Maine day — so clear we could see beyond Schoodic Point, all the way to Petit Manan. Whipped-cream clouds were heaped up in the translucent blue sky. Blue-green waves broke against huge rocks which were crowned by forests of spruce, pine, and fir. Beneath them grew another, miniature forest of silvery reindeer moss *(Cladonia rangiferina)* with other mosses of many shades and textures.

The pink-granite hillsides were etched with green and black lichen; in the crevices grew tiny, white-flowered strawberrylike potentilla. The sun was warm, and the scent of the sweet fern mingled with the fragrance of the forest. The wind had practiced bonsai on one juniper which was clinging to life at the edge of the sea, cutting it back again and again, twisting its branches and sweeping them across the rock.

We both spoke at once. "What an arrangement that would make!" Then we laughed

An Oriental figure
only 1 inch tall stands
beneath a 3½-inch "tree"
of reindeer moss.

Reindeer moss fastened to a miniature gnarled branch
makes a "bonsai" tree.

at each other for this was a flower arrangers' holiday. The scenery, the trees and flowers, the gulls wheeling in the sky, the little fishing villages — every pleasure was doubled for us. We not only enjoyed the actual moment of experience, but anticipated the future enjoyment when our memories would furnish inspiration for home decorations and flower-show exhibits reminiscent of our trip down the coast of Maine.

But inspiration alone is not enough, and from the moment we crossed the bridge at Kittery we started collecting the material with which to create the compositions we envisioned. Such treasure seeking (and finding) adds an extra thrill to any holiday.

Rug and mat by Elizabeth Kaufman.
Pottery by the Stokes and Denis Vibert.

AT KITTERY'S MAINE INFORMATION CENTER we received a folder entitled *Handcraft Trails in Maine*. This would be fun to follow; we might find some unusual flower containers and gifts for friends at home. Our first stop was at the Old Spalding Shop in South Thomaston where Elizabeth Kaufman (the editor of the folder) shows the work of the Maine Coast Craftsmen, including her own weaving.

Mrs. Kaufman specializes in wool carpets of a carefully planned "hit-or-miss" pattern, reflecting her fine sense of color. One rug of dark blue and maroon, with streaks of scarlet and light straw-yellow, appealed to us particularly. It was displayed with a collection of pottery which was harmonious in texture, quality, and color.

We thought of flowers and berries we had seen along the road. Their color seemed to have been woven right into the fabric: ferns just turning pale gold, so beautiful we had to stop and pick them to press (between the desk blotters under the suitcases which are standard car equipment for flower arrangers on their collecting trips); branches of wild cherries with their long, full bunches of fruit from yellow to red to maroon and almost black; clusters of brilliant red-fruited elderberry.

What an arrangement could be made of these materials to highlight the qualities of both rug and pottery. White yarrow would supply a strong accent through the center, and our latest discovery, "spiny sarsaparilla" (*Aralia hispida*), with its rounded seed-heads of pale yellow-green would give the needed height. We could envision the arrangement adding the finishing touch to this charming shop. For shops, like homes, are always made more charming by the inclusion of plant material in the scheme of decoration.

Here in Maine we had regained the early summer which had left New Jersey some three weeks before. Yarrow was still fresh and white. Dock ranged from green through pink to tan. Great masses of meadowsweet and steeple bush landscaped the roadsides. All these we picked to dry for winter use, along with the plushy heads of different rose-colored sumac.

The color range and variety in forms were ideal for an informal mass arrangement: long sprays of deep blue vetch, spikes of blue *Campanula rapunculoides* and violet Vervain, fluffy white Valerian and creamy Filipendula, the glossy leaves and good-sized single flowers of the deep pink rose, and the purple-flowering raspberry, which is a delight. Its star-shaped white calyxes remain after the petals have fallen and are almost more interesting than the flowers themselves.

When we reached our cottage, we were pleased to find many of our favorites growing nearby. The question of a suitable container was solved by the annual visit of the "Indian Lady" with her baskets, which the Akenabi (Penobscot) Indians make even today. Mrs. Cooper still goes to the swamps to pick the sweet grass whose fragrance is for us so nostalgic, reminding us of the sweet-grass sewing basket on Grandmother's bureau.

The bigger Indian baskets were made of split wood, with perhaps a bit of the soft, gray-green sweet grass for pattern as well as scent. Maine's flowers would certainly be happy in one of these.

ONE of the most enchanting places to visit in all of Maine is the Bird Shop of Wendell Gilley in Southwest Harbor. Here his carved and painted birds are displayed, each on its carefully selected piece of driftwood: a pompous puffin, a monkey-faced owl, upside-down chickadees, a bashful widgeon, a pink-legged stilt, scratching its ear.

Wendell Gilley is a self-taught artist, whose lifelong hobby of whittling has become a full-time profession. A third-generation plumber with no artistic training whatever, he recently sold his lucrative business and achieved his dream of making a living solely from his carving. No one seems able to resist his birds. They appeal to everyone, children and adults, fishermen and presidents — examples of his work are in the collections of ex-Presidents Truman and Eisenhower.

When we visited Mr. Gilley, he had just finished a group of sea gulls in various attitudes. They were perched on a long, sea-battered beam. We asked to complete their setting. From the collection of driftwood piled at the back door came a ridged "mountain" for the background. A wind-blown branch and a piece of the stunted pine so typical of the region framed the picture. Some sand and a few rocks in the foreground completed this impression of the Maine seacoast.

THE WORK OF THE POTTER DENIS VIBERT, seen at the Old Spalding House, has appealed to us greatly, and we soon visited his studio in West Sullivan. The loft of an old barn had been made into an attractive showroom. Shelves and tables of weathered boards were in keeping with the old beams and made an excellent background for the stoneware so tastefully displayed by Ruth Vibert.

There was one wall area of irregularly spaced shelves which would be ideal for a flower-show class entitled "Pottery Shop" — using plant material with ceramics in an over-all composition. To our great delight the Viberts allowed us to try out our ideas right there.

We selected pottery from all over the shop and placed it on the shelves: bowls, vases, plaques, candlesticks, and a female figure of most unusual character. All Vibert pots are thrown on the wheel, and this figure was made by that method, section by section: head, bust, arms, hands, and skirt. We were sure Mr. Vibert had put the final touches on the collar and hem while dreaming of New England's favorite dish. Had it been apple or cherry, we wondered.

Beside the symbol of New England womanhood is a large bowl of green apples and clusters of bright-red wild cherries. At the right is a group of blackened mullein stalks, silhouetted against the silvery beam. At the top of the shelves a tall pitcher holds sedge and day lilies. In the center is a bouquet of pearly everlasting and Queen Anne's lace.

26

Vibert stoneware in black and white, tan brown, and dull green seems made for
Maine's roadside flowers and fruits.

THE VIBERTS sold other things besides their own pottery, in particular the prints of Stell and Shevis: cards, calendars, handkerchiefs, scarves, and wall hangings. Many of the designs were inspired by nature; some were printed from blocks made of the actual plant material. Another flower-show class occurred to us — a class displaying materials, tools and/or the various steps followed in some particular craft. The work of Stell and Shevis would fit well into such a class.

We paid a visit to their studio on a quiet hilltop meadow west of Belfast. They greeted us with cordiality, even though they seemed somewhat puzzled at our interest in the mechanics of their art. They had had no more contact with flower arrangement than we had had with block printing.

After we had explained our newly aroused interest in craftmanship, they showed us their workroom with the stacks of original blocks. These were of deeply carved wood, colored by the inks used in printing, and were as decorative as the prints made from them.

Plenty of material here for a flower show, but also, what an addition to any home these blocks would be when used as wall decorations. The Shevises told us they had talked of covering a wall with their blocks at some time in the future. They kindly offered us the use of the gray barn door that formed a background wall of their studio on which we could display our selection.

We grouped together several blocks showing undersea subjects: the large, square "whirlpool" at the top; at the left, a vertical panel showing a waving sea plant with a sea horse beside it; a school of fishes at the bottom. Beside this grouping is driftwood with seaweed on it, sea fans, kelp, shells, and starfish, in a naturalistic arrangement.

Woodblocks
by Stell and Shevis.

28

Treasure Seekers' Return

UPON RETURNING HOME, we could hardly wait to unpack the lovely things we had found on our trip. First of all we unrolled the linen block print by Stell and Shevis. It showed the Nativity, but the personages and animals had been conventionalized and integrated into a panel with such interest of design that its use need not be limited to the Christmas season alone.

Its black and white, blue, gold, and terra-cotta were excellent against our cocoa-brown wall, and we hung it at once. What would best complement it? Blue hydrangeas would have matched the blue in the panel, but color was not the only consideration. There was also the need for strong, clean-cut form and dramatic contrast which the hydrangea did not have.

In our collection of Maine plant material we found tall, straight mullein stalks and the pressed, star-shaped, white leaves of the *Populus alba*. To match the black in the panel, we painted the mullein and also the wild sarsaparilla, whose delicate, radiating seed heads and thin angular stems supplied the necessary transition between the two stronger, contrasting plant forms.

A pair of arrangements were made to frame the Nativity, starting at the top with spikes of mullein. The white leaves were gradually worked into the vertical design, down to the low brown bowls, where they provided a strong focal area.

Many arrangers make a general statement, "light at the top — dark at the bottom." Like any general statement, this is debatable. It implies that dark material always looks heavy, and that light material always appears delicate. The real question is one of weakness or strength, which is governed not only by form, substance, and color, but also by the degree of contrast between the material and its background. Here the wall is dull brown. The contrast between it and the black mullein is less than that between it and the broad white leaves.

Block print by Stell and Shevis.
Pottery by Denis Vibert.

31

WHAT flower arranger has ever passed an antique shop without longing to stop and explore? Not these! So, of course, our treasures have been found in such shops as well as in the studios of contemporary craftsmen. By visiting both, we have come to a great appreciation of the artists who are carrying on the line of tradition from the past into the future — the tradition of man's making things with his own hands for his own use.

Today, when houses, furniture, utensils come off an assembly line, man must consciously desire to use his hands and mind in creative craftsmanship, and usually must fight the pressures of his environment to do so. Yesterday, every man — and woman — made things because he needed them to live. He was forced to create, to select his materials, fashion his tools, use the tools which he had made. Perhaps he was more fortunate than he knew; the deep satisfaction inherent in making something useful was a natural part of his everyday life.

Our antique shop finds included a wooden cranberry picker and a large scoop cut from one solid piece of wood, used, we were told, in mixing cottage cheese. They had both been made for a definite practical purpose which had dictated a simplicity of design most compatible with our modern room, and their age and long usage had merely added a pleasing natural patina. So we put them to a new use as flower container and accessory.

A six-foot branch of heavily berried firethorn (*Pyracantha*), selected for its angular shape, was placed in the cranberry picker in a diagonal position. Below the scoop, a group of squash, gourds, and white eggplants were placed in an old, pierced-tin foot warmer. A shorter spray of firethorn cut across the edge of the scoop and repeated in reverse the design of the large branch.

We hoped that those early toolmakers would have approved of this use. Although our aim was aesthetic rather than utilitarian, their utensils were once again filled with the fruits of the earth.

DELIGHTED with our discoveries on Maine's handcraft trails, we could not resist going home by way of the Guilford (New Hampshire) Fair, the oldest handcraft fair in the country. The quality and extent of the work shown was astonishing, including furniture, weaving, jewelry, enamels, and pottery. We had never visited such a fair, and had had no idea what it would mean to us as flower arrangers.

Like ours, the basic materials used — wood, metal, clay, wool, etc. — were from the natural world. And, being handmade, no two pieces were exactly alike, as are no two creations of nature. It was not surprising we should find so many containers and accessories just asking to be used with plant material.

One beauty suggests another. Form, texture, color, line — the distinctive qualities of a work of art — have the power to evoke in the perceptive mind a succession of related beauties, according to the beholder's background and interests. In our case, we saw a well proportioned, subtly colored bowl, and an almost tangible image formed itself before us — the bowl already filled with the ideal blossoms and foliage. Call it imagination, inspiration, or second sight, there seemed to be plenty of it wherever craftsmen congregated.

The craftsmen themselves (members of the League of New Hampshire Arts and Crafts) were responsible for the effective staging of the fair, and acted as salesmen, for everything on display was for sale. It added greatly to our enjoyment to meet and talk with the artists.

Our salesman, Bruce Epplesheimer, told us that many of his pots were designed especially for flower arrangement, and pointed out those so used by the local garden club women who had contributed their talents in the decoration of the exhibition. It was the first year for such collaboration. We found it most fitting, and hoped it would spread to other handcraft fairs throughout the country.

Glycerined catbrier, bayberry, and blueberry foliage are used in this composition. Catbrier follows the gently flowing contours of the flaring bowl, and casts delicate shadows on the table. The little bird sits beneath the berried branches. Bowl and bird by Bruce Epplesheimer.

35

ANOTHER ARTIST at the Guilford Fair, Gerald Williams, specialized in well formed, rough textured flower pots. We purchased one of his unique planters. A tall pot fitted inside an outer container whose cut-out sections created a bold, three-dimensional design.

The simplicity of this design called for strong line and silhouette in the material used in the pot. Two branches of cedar with pleasing, natural curves were held by a forked stick (one of the *kubari* used by the Japanese). This was wedged across the inside of the pot, an inch below the rim.

For a second arrangement, we selected branches of the lustrous coppery mahonia. The horizontal layers of leaves on the ends of the vertical, nearly bare stems repeat the angles of the container.

Due to the artlessness of these arrangements — they might almost be growing plants — they should give pleasure over a long period of time. One does not tire easily of natural beauty.

The fresh material used in all three arrangements in the Williams' planter could be treated with glycerine to make them permanent. The ends of the stems are crushed and placed in a solution of one-third glycerine and two-thirds hot water. After about two weeks in a cool place the leaves will have absorbed the solution and be ready for use. Complete submersion in a 50-per cent solution of glycerine and water is another method for preserving foliage of heavy substance such as mahonia, maple, oak, ivy, etc.

Glycerined material turns rich shades of brown but, unlike dried material, appears to be freshly cut and retains its shape, texture, and flexibility indefinitely. Even berries often absorb the solution and remain on the stems.

THIS PLANTER was, of course, made to hold a growing plant, and it would be an excellent container to use in bonsai, the 1000-year-old art of growing dwarf, potted trees. This is another expression of the intense appreciation felt by the Japanese for objects of nature, and is unique among their many contributions to horticulture throughout the world.

The aim is to catch the essence, rather than make a mere representation of nature. The potted trees are kept small by constriction and pruning of roots, severe pruning of upper branches and leaves, and special feeding and watering treatment. They are shaped by the pruning and by wiring.

Even starting at once, it would be years before we would have such a dwarfed tree. Meanwhile, we created our impression of this craft with the materials at hand.

In many examples of old bonsai, the trunk has become massive and gnarled, and out of all proportion to the spare, stunted branches and few green leaves growing from it. Here a heavy piece of bark-covered wood is the "trunk," the "branches" have been "pruned" by the wind and weather. Two pieces of arbor vitae are the foliage.

The Japanese say the best way to divest oneself of anger is to sit down before a bonsai in the making and trim it carefully, leaf by leaf. We feel that this value can be found in any work with plant material—including selecting, trimming, and arranging it.

Planter by Gerald Williams.

39

IN PARIS HILL, MAINE, we visited "Old Academy Handcrafts," the attractive shop of Peg and Larry Doore. Here was another couple who had established a business which gave them an outlet for their creative talents and the opportunity to live as they wished. Like the Viberts and the Shevises, the Doore's home shop was surrounded by the quiet beauty of the rural countryside, close to the fields, the woods, and the sea, which were a continual source of inspiration, as evidenced by their work.

We purchased a set of their brown and white table mats and napkins, and used them with pleasure, remembering the craftsmen and their way of life—an extra delight which comes with each piece of original handwork.

The table was set with plain white ware which continued the sharp contrast, without competing with the decorative pattern of the mats. For our centerpiece, we carried out the shell theme by selecting things that came from the sea, or looked as if they had. But, as there were so many shells on the mats, only one shell was used in the composition, to avoid overemphasis.

Two types of kelp and dried, spidery tropical leaves (*Jatropha texana*) form the main outline. At the center are brown and white Cecropia leaves and pods, and white, branching coral, all on a brown wooden base.

We enjoyed this table setting for summer lunches on the terrace, an added pleasure coming from the knowledge that the centerpiece would not be wilted by the sun, nor blown about by the breeze.

40

Table mats by Peg and Larry Doore.

41

Palm epergne by Reba Harris.

42

The Land of the Palm

AFTER OUR VACATION in Maine, any trip we took was enhanced by our new realization of the kinship among craftsmen, and how much the horizons of our own art could be widened by contact with the ideas of artists in other fields. The discovery of new viewpoints, like the discovery of new plant material, always brings fresh inspiration.

The trail we next followed was that of the palm—south to Florida, west to California and the Hawaiian Islands. There seemed to be no end to the variety of palm forms, and the uses to which they could be put.

Near the lovely little town of Eustis in Florida, a fascinating shop called the Garden Barn featured the native plant materials, both fresh and dried. The owner, Reba Harris, had developed an original variation of the ancient art of basketry, using the enormous flower tassel which falls from the sheath of the Queen palm (*Cocos plumosa*).

Section by section, around the strong center stalk, she wove a series of small, shallow baskets, making a many-tiered "epergne," a very unusual container and one most appropriate for colorful, exotic fruits and foliage: Pothos with tangerines, kumquats, immature pineapples, citron, Calamondin oranges, poisonous Ochrosia and edible Carissa fruits, small green bananas, and one star apple (*Averrhoa carambola*).

Much of the tropical material we found in Florida dictated its own use, not in flower arrangements, but as plant sculpture. The alternate, boatlike bracts of Traveler's Palm extending on either side of the upright stem make a satisfying design without any additions. We had only to place it in a suitable container—a boat-shaped palm sheath. Other than the removal of the lowest right-hand bract—to break the monotonous rhythm of the evenly spaced solids and voids—the material remained as it grew.

Modern sculpture has shown us the use of any material which comes to hand. Sometimes this is successful, sometimes it is not. The junk cultist, a commentator on one state of mind in our society, rejects the use of natural raw materials from which the artist once modeled or carved his own particular vision. Instead, he "assembles" torn cardboard, dirt-encrusted electric switches, drain pipes and doormats—factory made, via the rubbish heap.

No form in itself is ugly. Ugliness—or beauty—exists in the beholder's perception. When he says an object is beautiful, or ugly, it means that he receives from it sensations which satisfy some fundamental need or capacity, or sensations which dissatisfy.

But human perception is not an unclouded mirror, showing clear forms and colors. Every reflection is affected by other objects and feelings once associated with them in our experience. When recognizable articles are used as the basic elements of a piece of sculpture, these associations often outweigh the interest found in juxtaposition of form, color, and texture.

When the artist's avowed purpose is to shock—to create a non-art—it is not surprising to find his materials selected from man's outworn assembly-line symbols of sterility. Nor is it surprising that we, whose viewpoint is somewhat different, should prefer to use the forms of nature which, even after they have fulfilled their creative functions and been discarded, are still symbols of the life-giving force.

One of the most spectacular formations in Florida was the dried flower stalk of the Traveler's Palm (*Ravenala mada-gascariensis*), so-called from the clear, watery sap caught in the leaf sheaths, which afford a refreshing drink to thirsty travelers in arid regions. The tree grows twenty to thirty feet high, and the flower heads are three feet or more in length.

45

THE PALM LEAF is one of the commonest sights in the South and the West, but it is also one of the most fascinating, due to its dozens of variations in pattern, size, and shape. Some are featherlike plumes, others are flat, radiating, pleated fans, held on strong, thorny stalks seven or eight feet long.

The latter are six to eight feet in breadth, very unwieldy in their original state, and much too big for the hall in the modern home where we wished to put them. We cut away the outer portion, taking care to create an interesting, irregular outline. But there was no container big enough for this six-foot material.

Not for nothing had we been watching craftsmen. We took our courage in our hands and made a "planter" from wood blocks used in the printing of Japanese books. The black rectangles had the needed weight to hold the stylized leaf "trees."

The resulting dramatic simplicity demanded the minimum amount of accessory material. A giant digger pine cone (*Pinus Sabiniana*) and three sheaths of the Areca palm were placed at the base to break the rectangular areas formed by the three long, bare stems.

46

47

THERE IS SUCH AN ABUNDANCE of plant life in the tropics and semitropics that the exquisite design in even the commonest forms is often overlooked by those who see them every day. A newcomer to the area (a flower arranger, especially), seeing all the strange plants for the first time, finds the imagination stimulated and the urge to collect stronger than ever.

No rules of conservation were broken. Due to the prodigality of nature in warm climates, there is an excess of material of all kinds, but mainly from the many varieties of the palm. In piles of débris, waiting to be collected, there were great quantities of stalks from the Mexican palm (*Washingtonia robusta*).

From delicately curving branches grew smaller gnarled stems, branching again in nubby, wirelike strands which had held the fruit. One stalk placed on an Oriental base became an almost complete arrangement. However, the stem looked weak at the point of contact with the base, so a small palmetto fan was added for greater visual stability.

Other windfalls were the seed pods of the calico flower (*Aristolochia elegans*) which resemble small brown parachutes complete with cords, one from each of the six sections. These air-borne vessels were hung at irregularly spaced intervals on the palm stalk. Their radiating pattern and strong silhouette balanced and repeated the larger radiating design of the palmetto at the base.

Placed near an open window, the slightest breeze turned the composition into a dancing plant stabile.

48

49

Hawaii is truly the land of the palm since it is native there. But many other kinds of trees, less familiar to us, were of even greater interest: milo, monkeypod, koa, ohia, which provide material for some of the important industries. On the island of Kauai we saw a whole grove of ohia trees. The almost weightless wood is used, we were told, to make the floats for the outrigger canoes. The other woods, having most unusual grain, are made into trays, bowls, carvings, and furniture.

We had a firsthand look at the raw materials in a lumber yard outside Honolulu where tables of all kinds were being made. In the stacks of unfinished wood we found one burled end piece, grained with a flowing design in almost every gradation of brown, and with parts of the original bark still in evidence.

Having seen a sample of beautifully polished milo wood, we knew that this rough board, when finished and set on three sturdy legs, would make a unique coffee table. A large knothole at one side of the plank would provide a natural opening for a planter or a flower arrangement.

Home again in New Jersey, the completed table was a pleasant reminder of our journey. We further renewed our memories by setting in the planter an arrangement of red and pink anthuriums, typical of Hawaii, yet readily available from the florist even in our comparatively cold climate.

51

THE PLANT COLLECTOR does not have to be limited to dried or pressed material, but can also bring home growing things. Tropical plants which are not hardy outdoors can be grown on a window sill or in a greenhouse.

We brought back from California a pot of Spathiphyllum and a smaller spider plant (*Anthericum bichetii*). In the greenhouse this grew rapidly, sending out long, flowering sprays. At the end of each branch a leaf cluster developed which could be rooted for a new plant or used on its long, graceful stem in arrangements.

The pattern of the green-and-white striped leaves repeated that in our Nailsey flask, with its loops of white across the clear blown glass. To allow full play for the Anthericum's habit of growth, we placed the bottle on a hanging glass shelf. One branch falls below the shelf, the lowest "spider" being shown in complete silhouette, while the stem repeats the curve of the flask.

The material was placed in such a way that all lines lead the eye to the focal area, where they converge. We found that *Tradescantia fluminensis variegata*, and our Spathiphyllum from California were similar in design to the Anthericum, and provided the broader forms needed toward the center.

The Anthericum and Tradescantia will thrive for many weeks in a sunny window. The Spathiphyllum is long-lived, but will need to be replaced before the rest of the arrangement is gone.

No ONE ever comes back from the beach without a collection of shells. The question is what to do with them after you get them home. Remembering their beauty in the play of light and shadow through the shallow water on the Florida beach, we simulated the effect by arranging the shells and related plant forms behind the rippled surface of a pale aqua glass brick.

The resulting undersea study was used alone on a window shelf during the winter. In the summer it became an accessory with an arrangement.

Violet sea urchins, round in form and radiating in pattern, always remind us of blue-violet, round-headed Echinops. These were placed, with tall iris leaves, in a large glass brick where sand and shells (including the sea urchins) were swept across the bottom, like an ocean floor. Hoya tendrils, bearing shell-pink flowers, framed the glass-enclosed underwater picture.

FROM INLETS ALONG THE CALIFORNIA SHORE came our choicest pieces of weathered wood which had been "finished" by the wind and water. No matter how many one finds, no two are ever alike, and each one has its own characteristics. Some are purely decorative, suggesting trees blown by the wind; others have the added attraction of an amusingly recognizable likeness to a living creature of one kind or another.

One such free-form figure made us realize once more that nature was preferable to much modern sculpture. We mounted it on a burl and placed it in a tiny garden under the pine tree against the cypress fence. For its setting we made a pool of two half-oval, shallow copper pans.

Other treasures from the shore were stones, ground and polished by the sea. Those most useful to us were the small, flat, slate-gray disks and ovals found in great quantity on the Oregon coast. We made a pathway of these, placing them carefully in wet cement, following the broken curve of the pool.

An area of soil was left open behind each end of the pool for the needed planting: a small arbor vitae shrub at the right, Leucothoe at the left, with a pot of tulips for an immediate effect. Bulbs will be planted there for next spring.

At the base of the bushes are pieces of lava rock and in the small pool, for interest and balance, are three unusual gray and white stones, worn smooth and strangely pierced by nature.

Since the figure is removable, this garden spot can become a showcase for other natural or man-made sculpture which we may find on our journeys. Discovery and collection are one side of our pleasure, but an equal delight comes in using our finds, often combining those from many different parts of the world.

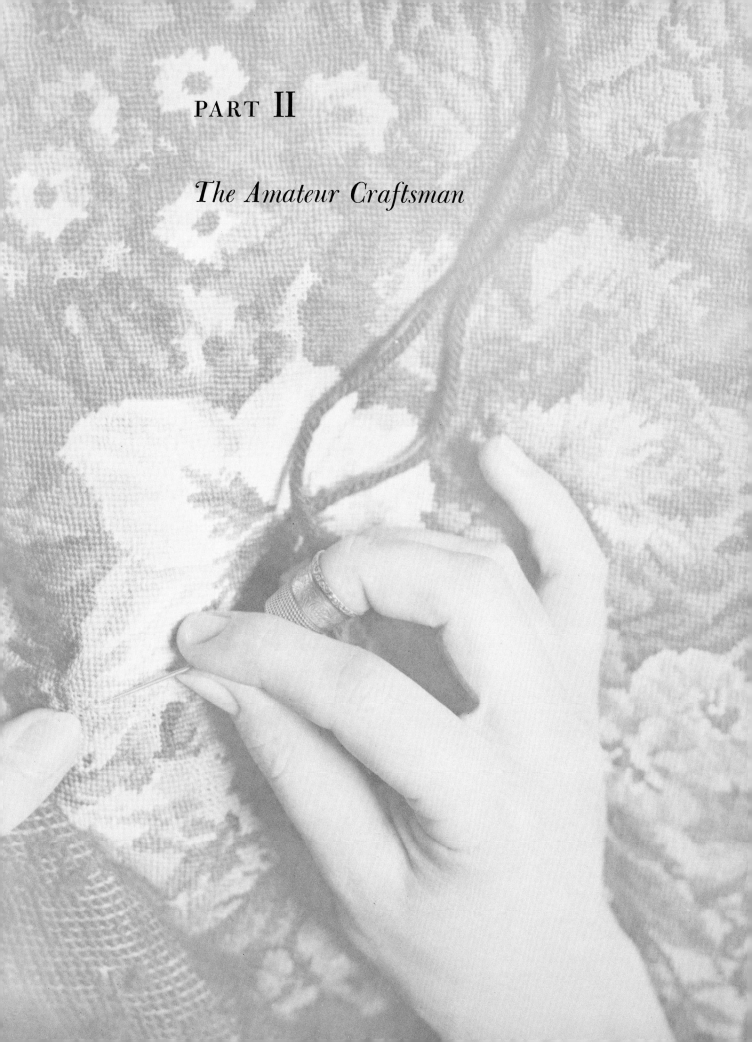

PART II

The Amateur Craftsman

Screens and Room Dividers

STIMULATED by the work of the craftsmen we had been meeting, we decided to experiment with ideas of our own, starting with the panels for a decorative screen. Such a screen provides a special setting for the plant material without which no room really comes to life. For this purpose a bold pattern should be avoided. An over-all, textural effect is preferable, as it does not compete with the compositions for which it is the background.

One way to create this textural effect is to make a "rubbing" as we did with pennies when we were children. By placing a piece of paper on any textured but fairly flat object, and rubbing it with charcoal, patterns appear as if by magic. Pastels can be used to give a more colorful but less contrasting pattern. Muted colors such as soft blue-green or green-yellow harmonize well with most plant material.

Surprising tracery can be made over a rag rug, tree bark, worn stair treads, metal grille work, woven fiber place mats, bamboo shades, or textured wallboards. Designs can be varied by the lightness or the heaviness of the pressure used when applying the charcoal, and by the direction or length of stroke — vertical, horizontal, diagonal, or circular, alone or in combination.

Our first rubbing was done with charcoal on white paper taped against an old, crudely cemented brick chimney. The pattern from the horizontal strokes alone was un-

interesting. But the addition of short, vertical strokes un-evenly applied over the horizontal strokes resulted in a design surprisingly reminiscent of Oriental brushwork.

In order to have unbroken lengths for our screen panels, we used a long roll of unglazed shelf paper. As soon as the rubbing of each section was completed, it was sprayed lightly with artists' fixative. Several applications were made until the charcoal no longer smeared when touched. The paper was then trimmed to size, and put on the wallboard panels of the screen with wallpaper paste.

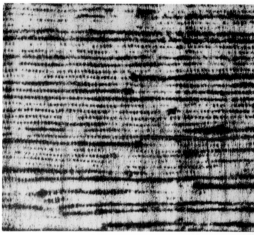

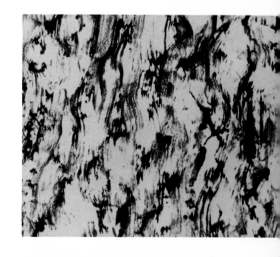

As soon as the screen was in place we realized it was an excellent background for our white Chinese figure for which we had had no worthy setting. She was first placed on a small table in front of the screen, but was overpowered by the expanse of pattern. The small table was replaced by a long, low one; the figure was raised on a tall stand, and a simple arrangement of small white narcissus and tulips was added as an accessory. Then the expanse of background was pleasantly spacious rather than overpowering.

IN THE SUMMER WHEN FLOWERS ARE ABUNDANT and colorful, we put away the white figure and use the screen as a setting for larger, more dramatic arrangements of fresh flowers. In one instance, brilliant red gladiolus and amaryllis with bright green Calla leaves in a dark copper bowl were placed on the small Chinese table. We found a line—or line-mass—arrangement was the most striking against the Oriental-modern screen.

IN OUR MAINE COTTAGE, the one large room is divided into various areas by two five-foot permanent screens. Two-by-fours make black frames around a series of white oblongs. One day a line arrangement of grass and wild sarsaparilla was placed on the bench in front of a panel. That night when the lights were turned on a shadow appeared on the screen, an almost perfect reproduction of the arrangement, giving us the idea to capture the design as a permanent decoration for the plain panel.

Using the children's paint brush, and the same brown paint with which the walls were covered, we followed the shadows, using quick, sweeping brush strokes. The results were so pleasing, and doing it such fun, that we—and the children—painted shadow pictures on the other panels, too. Single sprays of plant material were used rather than more arrangements, so they would not compete with the original design.

For a clearly duplicating shadow, the subject must be close to the background with the light directly in front of it and rather far away. For a large, blurry shadow the subject is moved away from the background and closer to the light, which may shine on it at an angle.

EVERYWHERE WE TRAVELED, we found fresh plants which were new and strange to us. We wanted to bring home specimens, and found their beauty could best be preserved by pressing. Such a collection can be used in many ways. Large sprays of foliage having good substance—like the *Populus alba* and Japanese maple—can be used in arrangements. Flowers and smaller leaves can be used to make flower "prints," greeting cards, place cards, and tallies, or can be embedded in liquid plastic for boxes, paperweights and screens.

We found an even easier method was to glue the material to a thin oblong sheet of plastic, then cover it with another sheet of the same size, and fuse the two together with acetone or plastic cement. To display a number of such panels, a simple room divider was constructed from slender pieces of wood.

Each small panel was hung from a cross strip by two S-shaped hooks formed from a piece of heavy wire. These were inserted in the panels through two holes drilled at the upper corners. Alternate openings were left empty to give each panel emphasis and to create a more interesting over-all pattern.

In this one screen we can follow our travels: from Maine's tiny, wild green orchid and star-shaped purple-flowering raspberry, through Florida's flower of the silk-oak tree (*Grevillea robusta*) and California's wild iris and Penstemon, to the tiny ferns which are the first green things to appear in the lava beds after the eruption of an Hawaiian volcano.

The panels can easily be changed if we bring home new gleanings from future travels, as we know we will—whether we journey to the Greek Isles or merely to our own back yard.

Room-divider frame by Harold Brooks

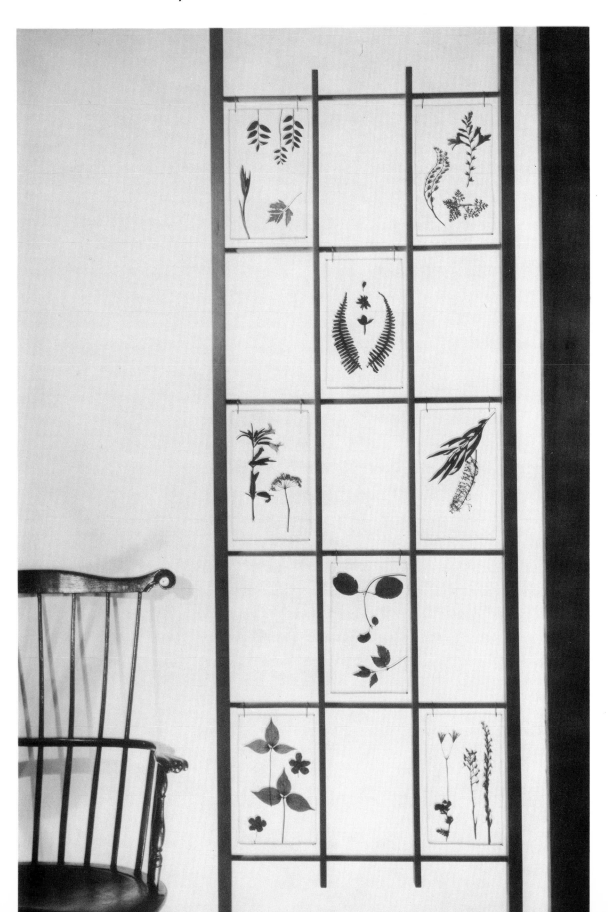

69

OVERSPECIALIZATION in flower arrangement, as in other arts, is a narrow road that is likely to lead to a dead end. Our new interest in the crafts widened our field of vision, opening the broad paths of fresh inspiration.

Reading articles in the magazine *Craft Horizons* we had become enamored of the woven paintings in which artists had used a needle to weave across an open warp in defining the subjects: a man's head, a bird, a fantastic tree.

We decided to make one for ourselves, using actual, glycerine-soaked grass as part of the design. Not having a loom, we made a frame of wood, with tacks set closely together all around the four edges. The warp was strung from top to bottom, with openings left for the grass, which was set in as part of the warp.

The weft was woven with a needle, over and under the grass-and-string warp, and around the tacks on the sides of the frame. Areas of the weft were left open to balance the solid areas of the warp. When this was finished, the tacks were driven into the frame, and covered by a narrow strip of wood. Fastened to two uprights, the panel made an unusual room divider.

The informality of the subject called for a naturalistic use of plant material rather than an arrangement. On the chest under the weaving a large, solid grouping of foliage plants (an Episcia and a Maranta) in a gnarled root supplied the needed weight below the panel and softened the rectangular shape of the frame. The curves of the root repeat the design of the leaves in the weaving.

Woven panel by Mary Alice Roche.

72

Wall Decorations

FLOWER ARRANGERS have been practicing a special craft for some time — using the materials of nature to make three-dimensional wall decorations instead of the usual free-standing compositions.

Seeds, pods, and pressed flowers are most often seen, but shells and other sea forms lend themselves to such use. Remembering the shell work of our grandmothers' day, Victorian frames seemed appropriate, but plain rather than ornate ones were selected as being in character with the planned design.

The same principles followed in flower arrangement are the guide in making shell pictures. The basic pattern is established with curving twigs or sections of sea fan, and developed with various sizes, shapes, and kinds of shells. These have enchanting names: murex, coquina, limpet, angel wing, kitten's paw, bubble, star, and jingle shell (or baby's footprint). All material is fastened to the pale-green matboard background with jeweler's adhesive.

The predominately brown-and-white color scheme in the framed pictures is carried out in the permanent arrangement of dried moth-mullein seed stalks and bush clover (*Lespedeza capitata*), glycerined beech leaves, pressed *Populus alba* leaves, and white branch coral — all on a burl base.

TREASURE SEEKING is not limited to far-off places. The attic of the old homestead — where we found the frames for our shell pictures — is often as good a source as any antique shop.

Even after the turn of the century much work was done by hand, and the pleasures of leisure were found in handwork, too. Well brought-up young ladies did needlework and china painting. Surprisingly, one member of our family had taken up the rather masculine art of wood carving, creating her own designs to decorate furniture and make wood panels.

In the attic we found a panel which showed acanthus leaves and chrysanthemums in high relief. It made an unusual wall decoration, and was also an accessory strong enough to use with an arrangement of flowers in the good-looking pottery bowl we had found at the Guilford Fair.

Five large chrysanthemums follow the edge of the plaque. The two elements are united into one composition by this placement, by the similarity of plant material in both — gently curving leaves and flower petals — and through the dominant-subordinate relationship of the arrangement and the panel.

Although the two parts are from different "periods," there is an affinity in surface interest and substance, a feeling of unusual visual weight and strength in the thick wood, the heavy pottery, and the sturdy flowers.

Today we realize that one need not be limited to combinations of things associated with the same place or the same period of time — unless the association is so strong it outweighs everything else. Usually the relationship of the inherent physical qualities of the actual objects is of first importance.

Plaque by Vesta Curtis Candor. Bowl by James McKinnell.

CHILDREN OF TODAY are given more freedom of artistic expression than were those of the early nineteen hundreds. The routine sewing a fine seam has been replaced by other occupations more stimulating to the imagination (if not necessarily producing an equal mastery of technique).

Two of our young friends like to cut out and paste. One year, after a vacation in the country, they produced a rural scene: hills, valleys, house, barn, animals, and a many-rayed sun. Then they decided that this farm must have crops.

Children also enjoy seeing plants grow; at any time of year, and even in the city, this pleasure is easily available. Tops cut from carrots, turnips, beets, and parsnips will produce green leaves when placed in a saucer of water. Grapefruit, lemon, and orange pits will grow into little trees when planted in pots of soil.

To achieve the effect of a realistic farmland in front of the picture, such sprouted vegetables were used as clumps of "trees" and "bushes" in a long shallow pan. Rows of "vegetables" were made from tiny weeds which are always springing up around house plants. A path of white sand wanders across the field to the opening in the fence.

76

Cut-out-and-paste farm
by Susie and Debbie Lewis, aged 5 and 8.

THE UNPARALLELED LIFE AND ART OF ANCIENT EGYPT have always captured our imagination, but there are few art objects available which could be used as accessories to an arrangement inspired by this period in history. In a book on Egyptian tomb painting we found pictured two panels of hieroglyphics framing a figure of the goddess Isis. These were different from the usual flat wall paintings. They were raised in gold on a brown background, an effect which could be reproduced in metal.

Our projects often involve other members of the family. In this case, a co-operative husband outlined decorative hieroglyphics on a sheet of copper foil. It was placed on a soft surface and the design was raised by pressing and stretching it with tools used in leatherwork — first from the back, then finished on the front. The metal was antiqued by submerging in a solution of liver-of-sulphur. When dry it was polished lightly to produce gold high lights on the raised portion, then mounted on an off-white board.

When it was hung on the wall we made a companion piece to carry out the Egyptian legend. "Through the high blue, in the Atet boat, sails Ra the sun god. His and tulip seed pods symbolize the sun, lotus, bird, and serpent motifs recurrent in Egyptian legend. "Through the high blue, in the Atet boat, sails Ra the sun god. His guiding snake is on his forehead."

"Awake, sleepers!
Before the great bittern
That hast risen up out of the Nile . . .

Awake in peace, Harakhti, in peace!
Thou sleepest in the Barque of the Evening,
Thou awakest in the Barque of the Morning."

From the Old Kingdom texts,
2600 B.C. or earlier.

78

Copper panel by Harold Brooks.

THE RUBBING TECHNIQUE used to make our four-fold screen was also employed in creating an inexpensive set of scrolls. These were especially designed to supplement our favorite types of arrangements when natural materials alone were not adequate to fill a large wall space.

A circular design is a good contrast for the mainly vertical arrangements. For this we used a flat, round wooden mat from Denmark, made of sticks set on edge with wooden beads threaded between the sticks to hold them in place.

The mat was placed under a length of shelf paper, in first one position and then another. Each time the mat was moved to a new position under the paper, charcoal was rubbed over it in a circular motion, with varying degrees of pressure. Sometimes the whole was rubbed in, sometimes the outer edge alone, or portions of it. The center was used to make circles of gradually decreasing size.

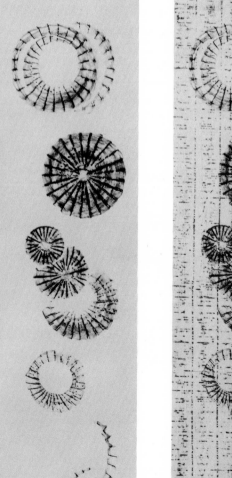
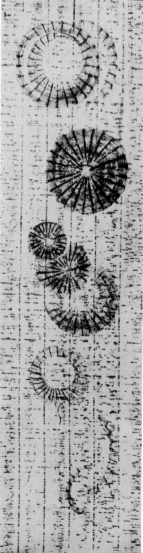

The result was unrelieved contrast and demanded comparable arrangements such as a black container holding tall branches of dark and light striped okra, with clusters of agave pods at the base.

But when we made an arrangement of pink Japanese flowering quince we found it too delicate for the stark circles, so we softened them by placing the scroll over a matchstick curtain and rubbing it lightly down the length with charcoal. The finished effect was Oriental in feeling and in keeping with the line arrangement of flowering branches.

Pressed ferns provided the pattern for another scroll, this to be used with naturalistic arrangements of weathered wood and wild flowers. An ash tray shaped like a fish and a branch of Queen palm provided the pattern for a scroll to be used with undersea treasure — sea fans, shells, etc.

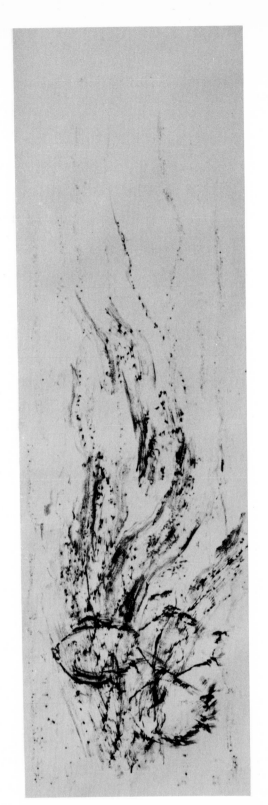

Care was taken to rub only that part of the paper directly over the object being used to make the design. And, of course, each scroll was sprayed with fixative as soon as finished, but not before, as the paper will not take any more charcoal after it has been sprayed. To finish, the scroll was glued to two black dowels and hung by a black cord.

THE FIRST SCROLLS were all done in black and white. In the tulip season we tried some color. We started with the background, placing the length of paper on the broadloom-twist carpet, then rubbing the surface of the paper with chartreuse pastel, first in one direction and then in another, until the whole appeared to be evenly textured. The paper was then placed over the matchstick curtain, and the tulips were drawn on it in greens and pinks.

An arrangement of deep-pink tulips in a dark green bottle was related to the scroll in material and design, but when the two were put together the effect was not pleasing. The scroll was large in size but weak in color and substance, while the arrangement was smaller in size but strong in color and substance and more dramatic in outline. The result was a division of the whole picture into two areas of interest which were equal in visual impact, thus creating competition between the two parts rather than the desired harmony of a unified whole.

We replaced the arrangement of tulips in a bottle with a larger, weightier one of wisteria branches and tulips, which became the dominant feature of the composition while the scroll became the subordinate accessory. The horizontal black base under the container repeated the line and color of the two thinner black wooden rods which held the scroll.

83

NEEDLEWORK has always been a classic homecraft for women. Today it is having a renascence as an artcraft, using old techniques for new effects. Marion Rowley, expert needlewoman, gardener, flower arranger, and art enthusiast, has still another interest. From the flowers and herbs in her own garden she makes potpourri of ineffable fragrance.

Combining her hobbies, she designed and stitched a wall decoration using appliqué as the method and materials of potpourri as the subject matter: oranges and limes struck with cloves, stick cinnamon, sweet woodruff and lemon verbena, nutmeg with its fanciful overlay of mace, Calamus root, and of course the basic rose.

Beneath it on the table, in an old knife box, is piled fruit in repetitive form and color: osage oranges, persimmons, pomegranates, quinces, nutmegs, and pomander balls. No foliage obscures the clean-cut outlines.

At the right is an arrangement of cattails, milkweed pods, rose hips, rhododendron leaves, quinces, tangerines, and dried orange-peel "flowers." Forms and colors repeat those in the panel.

This kind of composition is not only an exercise in design. Through association it also tells of one gardener's ever-widening fields of interest and illustrates how the creative imagination draws upon the many facets of experience.

Nutmeg, with its fanciful overlay of mace.

Appliqué hanging by Marion Rowley.

86

Rug by Betty Ericsson.

Rugs, Furniture, and Architectural Features

ANOTHER OLD CRAFT in which there has been continued interest is that of rug making. Hooking is probably the most popular method, offering opportunity for subtle and realistic shadings of color according to the width of the strips of material used.

The interests of the rugmaker naturally influence greatly the choice of pattern. Betty Ericsson, being a gardener, chose leaves as her inspiration, dyed her material, and blended her colors with the actual plant material before her.

In the fall, when the rug was finished and placed before the hearth, a large arrangement at one side of the fireplace repeated many of the colors and plants. An old red-leather fire bucket was used as a container. Sumac in tones of soft yellow through red, dried tan magnolia leaves, red blueberry leaves, and red and yellow heads of dried cockscomb were arranged against the blue wall.

Before MASS PRODUCTION took over the work formerly done by the family craftsman, his need to make the children's playthings himself led to individuality in toys and furniture.

Many of our most cherished heirlooms are such pieces, made by loving fathers for unspoiled sons and daughters. Unhampered by inhibitions regarding his inability to compete with factory-produced goods, he followed his own ideas, finished each item to the best of his ability, and took joy in his children's happiness when they received his unique gift. This joy — and this relationship between father and child — is not deliverable from the factory.

The possession of such a legacy, a sturdy little chair which must have pleased many generations of children, inspired a modern father to make his daughter a small table as a companion piece. Adapting a 17th-century design, the table was made in style and proportions to suit the chair.

The two pieces sat beside an enormous fireplace. In the summer, as a tribute to our friends, we made a pair of arrangements — a small bouquet of mixed wild and garden flowers on the table, and a large bouquet on the left in an old stoneware jar.

Table by Edward R. Candor.

90

A WORK OF ART can be produced by an individual talent, or by a tradition. Within the tradition of building his own home and hearth the ordinary man once developed the skills and inherited, almost unconsciously, the cumulative knowledge needed to become a fine craftsman.

Today, in our civilization, only the extraordinary man thinks of trying for that satisfaction, and he must work out for himself a set of personal skills and values to take the place of that common inherited knowledge which we have largely lost.

In the past a fireplace, for instance, was a necessity and was built with its utilitarian purpose in mind rather than as an artistic endeavor. Yet it often resulted in aesthetic pleasure through the traditional craftsman's inherent feeling for functional beauty.

In the upstairs bedroom of the eighteenth-century home of the C. J. Owens, the confluence of three flues and the position of the window under the slanting roof dictated an unusual chimney line and an asymmetrical placement of the fireplace. Within the physical restrictions, the builder created a workable heating unit — and a bold pattern of light and dark delineated by horizontal, vertical, and diagonal lines of various lengths.

It is a particular pleasure to decorate a room which thus combines interest of design, history, and human association. The large area of white at one side of the plain fireplace opening made an excellent background for a tall, permanent arrangement of treated materials: rough, dried bush clover and the near-black, smooth, glycerined foliage of copper beech, catbrier, and blueberry.

A LIVING TRADITION is a compatible combination of the old and the new, rather than complete preoccupation with one and complete rejection of the other. In building a modern kitchen in an old house, the owner with imagination retains as much as possible of the original features — particularly such outstanding ones as a Dutch oven and a fieldstone wall.

In this corner of the C. J. Owen kitchen, the wall and oven set the theme. Near the oven hangs a round, wrought-iron rack, holding old iron cooking forks. Below it is a many-drawered storage chest which held, according to the labels: salt, starch, hominy, barley, and wheat.

A studied arrangement would be quite out of place in the informal atmosphere of this early American kitchen corner. Casual arrangements of gourds and corn in a bowl in the Dutch oven and sheaves of grain in a wooden measure are suitable in type and spirit to the room and the house.

Accessories

THE WORD "AMATEUR" comes from the Latin verb *amare* meaning to love. In other words, the amateur craftsman is one who works purely for the love of his craft. He can make what he wants without concern for the market appeal and value, and he can take as much time — and work as painstakingly — as he wishes to develop his ideas, without worrying about a deadline and the cost of his man-hours.

And the amateur with an inquiring mind can venture into any field which presents itself as a challenge. Such a one is Douglas Withers, amateur craftsman extraordinary — photographer, weaver, furniture maker, sculptor, among other things. Each craft was pursued until he had completed a particular project to meet his own high standards.

Inspiration could come from anything. When clearing a site for a new home, the bole of an old pine tree reminded him of an eagle carved by the 19th-century artist, Wilhelm Schimmel. He decided to carve an eagle for himself, thus adding wood sculpture to his list of interests. The result was a very large, very dramatic, stylized bird which held the place of honor on the extended mantel shelf in the living room.

The tremendous impression of strength given by the eagle required a container and plant material of comparable visual weight to go on the hearth beneath. The thick, pointed, outer leaves of an overgrown heirloom century plant (*Agave Americana marginata*) were placed to extend upward and outward into space. Distorted leaves repeat the shape of the eagle's wings.

Available flowers were too weak in substance for use with this heavy plant, but, in pulling out the leaves, we noticed the unusual white enlargements at the ends. These "spoons," used as flowers, became a strong accent through the center of the design, and repeated the white borders on the edges.

94

Carved eagle by Douglas Withers.

The large eagle with its companion arrangement had great dramatic impact but, because of its size and style, could only be used in a certain type of setting. On the other hand, a spot can always be found for a "miniature."

On the desk in the den, with books of the sea and a seedling spruce planted in a bowl, a tiny fishing wharf reminds us of our Maine vacation. It was whittled, not by a craftsman, but by an enthusiastic fisherman and lover of the sea (and a daily visitor to the shop of Wendell Gilley, bird carver). In a moment of nostalgia he had been moved to recreate his favorite scene, although he had never before done work of this kind.

The little shack on its dock, with lobster pots, bait barrel, and boat — all in scale — is completely captivating. We could scarcely wait for the next flower show where, in a small niche, we created in miniature, a bit of the Maine coastline. The fishing wharf was set on a piece of driftwood resembling rock and water. In back of it rise three "pointed firs" made from bracken pinnules.

96

Fisherman's wharf by Jack Roche.

Metal tray by Fred Loiseaux
Ceramics by Mrs. Walter Swain

98

THE INCENTIVE TO CRAFTSMANSHIP can come in many ways: from the desire to make something that is needed, to display treasures in an unusual way, to try something new, or to do something we see someone else doing and enjoying. Being one of a family of craftsmen should provide the strongest incentive of all.

Mr. Fred Loiseaux has for many years made hammered-copper, pewter-washed bowls and trays. Although inspired by the magnificent metalwork of the East, he develops his own designs with their intended use in mind. His wife is an ardent flower arranger and the distinction of her compositions is greatly enhanced by her husband's handiwork.

His daughter, Mrs. Walter Swain, is a flower arranger like her mother and a craftsman like her father. Her three children are being brought up to follow in the family tradition. Mrs. Swain's forte is ceramics, mainly flower containers which she uses in her home and in garden club work.

Like any true ceramist, Mrs. Swain rejects the use of production-line molds which destroys rather than encourages the development of the creative imagination. When a mold is needed, she carves her own from plaster of Paris, making a convex shape so the clay can be laid over the form, or a concave shape into which the clay is pressed. The latter method was used in making the fruit compote. For a rectangular container, slabs for sides and bottom are cut and modeled directly from the clay.

A grouping of the work of Mr. Loiseaux and his daughter resulted in a combination of straight and curved lines, patterned and plain surfaces. This suggested an arrangement in which the strong linear pattern of Echinops stems emphasizes the squareness of the container, while the supplementary branches follow the lines of the tray and compote. There is likeness between the symmetrical design of the flower heads and the embossed pattern on the tray, as there is between the smooth surfaces of leaves and containers.

Tomorrow's Craftsmen

M RS. SWAIN'S DAUGHTERS are fortunate in being members of a family which realizes the rich rewards of the creative use of hand and mind. But all children should have such opportunities, in school if not at home.

We were pleased to see, in our home town, an exhibit of work done by the students in the local high-school arts-and-crafts class. An entire window in a local department store, J. M. Towne & Co., was turned over to the class by the public-spirited owner. There were rugs, hangings, and ceramics displayed on shelves made of weathered wood.

We were allowed to add related plant material. Below the burlap hanging which shows a stylized tree and sun, a container with a barklike surface holds a rough, twisted branch. A variety of cones and nuts make a central grouping. Other cones on a branch are in a container which, we were later told, had itself been inspired by the form of a pine cone.

The teacher, Pete J. Carr, says, "We see in the pineapples, acorns, nuts, pine cones, and other seed pods the consummate forms that nature has devised as containers. These functional designs we translate into containing vessels of clay. Since clay has an inherent beauty of its own, we usually avoid covering it completely with glaze, but allow some of the basic material to show through."

The last principle was carried out in a pot with alternate bands of glazed and unglazed surfaces. In this container we used the glossy brown seed pods of Heracleum with golden heads of cotton grass (*Eriophorum viridicarinatum*), carrying out in color, texture, and association their relationship to their common origin, the earth.

Jar by Glenn Olson

Rug by Dorothea Morris. Hanging by Carol Starke. Ceramics by Arlene Meyer, Dorothy Cowan, George Stagg, Tom Harrington, Anna Marie Messina, and Glenn Olson. Work done in the arts-and-crafts class of Grover Cleveland High School, Caldwell, N. J.

101

THE QUALITY of tomorrow's craftsmen depends in a large part on today's teacher and his approach to the subject of craftsmanship. He must have formulated a personal philosophy and then be able to communicate it to the students.

Mr. Carr's philosophy stems from respect for natural materials and the joy of working with them — as, of course, does ours. We were both interested to discover that the forms from which he draws his inspiration are the actual medium in which we work. He uses clay and glaze to make his nature-inspired designs; we use the natural substance of living plant material.

In his studio Mr. Carr had set up a display of his own ceramics, paintings by his students, and a wood design in space by his wife. In a large hearth bowl we made a tall arrangement of Strelitzia and ti leaves, with *Philodendron warscewiszii* and one sculptured Echeveria. In this combination of our two crafts it was obvious how each enhanced the other.

The exhibition in the department-store window and our subsequent meeting with Mr. Carr seemed to have resulted in a widening of horizons for both of us. Certainly, seeing the work he was doing with his pupils had been a happy experience for us, affirming our belief that the deeply satisfying world of craftsmanship should be opened to more and more children in more and more schools across the country.

Ceramics by Pete J. Carr. Wood design by Marilyn J. Carr.
Painting by Virginia Murdock.

PART **III**

The Designer-Craftsman

The First Craft

TODAY the word "craft" is generally applied to work done in three dimensions and primarily planned for use. The designer-craftsman is one who executes his own designs. According to this definition, nature would be the first, and greatest, craftsman. Everything in the natural world seems designed and executed for its own continual recreation and that of the entire interrelated complex of life.

An important part of this complex is the family of grasses. These form the prairies and steppes of the world. With its enormous root system (378 miles of roots, 6000 miles of root hairs on one 20-inch plant of winter rye), grass covers the soil — protecting it against the erosive forces of wind and water — in arid regions where other plants cannot survive.

The more than 10,000 species of grasses and sedges provide food for animals, many of which provide food for man. And for more than 5000 years grasses have been cultivated to become man's "staff of life." These plants are adapted for wind pollination and do not have brightly colored flowers. Their appeal to the eye lies in line and rhythm.

In studying a single stalk or plant of grass, we see that nature, while creating it for a utilitarian purpose, has also produced a finished design of great integrity, which needs no rearrangement by us. It cannot be improved upon. The role of the flower arranger is, first, the recognition of the natural beauty of the material and, then, its placement in a suitable container, with compatible accessories if desired.

Carex sedge.
Right: Foxtail grass. Heron by Wendell Gilley.

Flowers have an infinite variation in size, shape, color. Some are enormous. Some, like the flowers of grass, are so small they pass almost unnoticed. Others have a large spathe which is commonly called a flower, though the myriads of tiny true flowers are on a spadix hidden inside the sheath.

Among the more familiar of these aroids are: skunk cabbage, Calla lilies, philodendron, and Jack-in-the-pulpit. The last, like grass, is effective when used alone in its original state. We placed companion plants in two bowls, taking care to emphasize the profiles of each pulpit and its Jack.

Each living organism was designed to reproduce its kind, but within this purpose each one has many functions, as each is dependent upon the others in what is known as the food chain. This is a continuing process of life where soil feeds the living plant and the dead plant replenishes the soil; where the animal eats the grass but fertilizes the soil that provides food for the grass, etc.

The more than 80,000 species of fungus have the job of breaking down dead matter so it will not encumber the earth but be returned to it as food for future generations of plants.

Every growing thing casts its own particular spell. In the curious forms, colors, substance, taste, and mythological associations of mushrooms and other fungi, there is a strange, sublunary magic.

Bowls by Denis Vibert.

Fungi

Vase by the Stokes.

112

Primitives

NATURE, THE CRAFTSMAN, must have been very pleased with certain plant forms which have been allowed to exist since their beginnings in the dim past without being changed by evolution. These are called primitive plants. They include horsetail rushes, cycads, and the familiar ginkgo tree, which Darwin called "the living fossil," as it was abundant in the time of the dinosaur.

Today we look with amazement at this form which appears to have reached the highest stage of culture, yet grows in the same form in which it grew millions of years ago.

In examining a single branch, we notice the alternate, stubby stems from which the leaves spring. These stems are made of woody layers, one of which is added each year as new leaves develop, grow, and fall. They are most noticeable in the spring when the fan-shaped leaves (from which comes the common name of maidenhair tree) are very small. At this time, each exquisite leaf whorl stands out in silhouette.

Two angular branches of this prehistoric ginkgo tree have been placed in an unglazed pottery cylinder container upon a footed burl. The natural formation of the material, unchanged by us, dictated the asymmetrical design.

SOME CRAFTS OF PRIMITIVE MAN, like the primitive forms of nature, have not changed greatly since their beginnings. In some places in the tropics primitive bark cloth is still made from the inner bark of the paper mulberry (*Broussonetia papyrifera*) which bleaches white, various ficus which dry dark brown, and the breadfruit tree (*Artocarpus incisa*) which dries light brown.

The outer bark is scraped off with a shell, the inner strips are soaked in water and then beaten out on a flat, hollow log. The better cloth was decorated with patterns, sometimes painted, sometimes printed by pressing on it leaves of flowers dipped in dye—or a block made by stitching pieces of midribs of palm leaves onto another leaf in a geometric pattern. Such tapa cloth was used for clothing, bedclothes, and wall drapery, in religious ritual, and as a symbol of wealth.

When using a tapa pattern as a background for an arrangement, we were governed in our choice of plant material by both the design and the geographical origin of the cloth. We used a combination of curving and angular forms from the tropics: a pineapple top, Yucca leaves, and Strelitzia flowers and leaves against an upright, shieldlike palm spathe.

A series of woven fiber mats, hung in a geometric pattern, provide a plain background which sets off the plant grouping from the strong, compelling rhythm of the design in the fabric.

PRIMITIVE MAN is pre-eminently religious. All his values of life—from food to sculpture and the observations of the stars—are primarily religious interests.

Naturally, his skill as a craftsman is employed in the making of ritual objects. Tribes of New Guinea carved—pierced and incised—and painted intricate patterns on this Gopi board and the dance shield which was used in ceremonial rites. The food bowl with the carved projections came from the Admiralty Islands.

To the savage, plants, animals, and inanimate objects can be endowed with mana, the power affecting man for better or worse, while totems (which serve as the sign of clan relationship) are chosen not only among animals, plants, and inanimate objects, but even abstract qualities like "pride." There are "split" totems such as the tongue of an animal; "cross" totems are the ends of things; and "linked" totems comprise a number of things.

Although we did not know just what sacred things inspired the artist in making these conventional designs, there were obvious likenesses to familiar plant forms: strangely "carved" and convoluted embryo palm; pierced lotus pods; sharp, pointed artichokes and young pineapple; round forms of various fruits, and a mature pineapple with curving leaves and "incised" surface pattern. These are combined as the symbols of an imaginary linked totem.

Photographed in the Newark Museum, N. J.;
Curator of Ethnological Art, Hunter Ross.

116

Folk Art

FOLK ART is the making of utilitarian objects by and for the ordinary people in small towns and villages, working within an indigenous tradition which remains basically unchanged over generations. It is a craft art in which—as in that of children and primitive civilizations — modern man finds an unself-consciousness and an honesty of purpose which is refreshing and appealing.

Basketry has always been one of the most popular of folk crafts. Archeological remains indicate that it was fully developed some 3000 years ago. In Japan, baskets are still used in the daily tasks as containing vessels. Since the 16th century they have been used in the tea ceremony, wherein emphasis is put on the beauty of everyday objects.

We like to think that the two bamboo baskets brought to us from the Orient might have been used in such a ceremony. However, we were not restricted by Japanese tradition in making our arrangements but were, instead, governed by the physical characteristics of the containers and their setting.

We hung one basket which had a handle made from a gnarled and twisted branch. Below, and to one side, we placed the urn-shaped basket which stood on three small feet.

Curving sprays of golden forsythia, arranged informally, led the eye from one container to the other, resulting in an integrated over-all design. One large scarlet flower of day-blooming cereus (*Phyllocactus*) balances the red-lacquer stand and sets off the whole composition.

118

Bowl by Denis Vibert
Cylinder vase by the Stokes.

122

TODAY, IN JAPAN as elsewhere in the world, folk craft has almost died out due to the competition of modern machine production. At the same time contemporary artists have been profoundly influenced by folk art. Some have returned to traditional techniques and designs, while creating original work in their own style.

Among these are the modern folk dyers. They work extensively with textiles, but their greatest success has been with sets of paste-dyed paper calendars which reflect their interest in the Japanese scene, its flowers and its folk customs. These calendars are so striking that they remain decoratively pleasing even after their intended usefulness has passed.

Arrangements were made to accompany representatives of the four seasons. Poinsettia stalks and true flowers without the brilliant bracts repeat the angles of January's gate into the new year. Anemones complement May's calendar, copper Cotoneaster and yellow yarrow the one for October.

July's calendar shows bamboo hung with strips of colored paper on which characters are written. This is in reference to *Tanabata*, the celebration on the seventh day of the seventh month of the meeting in the sky of the two stars representing the mythological weaver girl and her herd-boy lover. On this day poems are hung on bamboo which is set up in the garden with festive food spread beneath it. In the evening after the food is eaten, the poem bamboo is taken to the stream and tossed in. This was believed to bring skill in weaving as well as to guarantee good crops. Today *Tanabata* has become merely a festival for children, and it is this aspect which is reflected here.

In the Italian Tyrol wood carving is the traditional folk art. The Tyroleans being a Catholic people, much of their work depicts the pageant of the Nativity. A distinctive charm lies in the fact that the artist models his figures from the country folk of his own region, as if the ageless story were taking place in his own town and time.

We could not resist one particular group including two girl children angels and three true shepherds. Here realistic characterization has been sublimated to express the very spirit of adoration. For these peasant figures we made a naturalistic setting of moss-covered rocks. From the stone springs the miraculous Christmas rose.

124 *Trolls…from Sweden, the land of wooden toys*

Who comes tromping over our bridge?" said the trolls.

Museum Visits

MUSEUM VISITING has long been one of our favorite holiday pastimes, but after our contacts with craftsmen—and owning and using their work as well as trying some of our own—we looked with greater understanding and deeper enjoyment at all the exhibits. And, of course, a museum is the place to see the very finest examples of craftsmanship practiced through the ages.

In this day of shortened distances, almost everyone can take advantage of the many fine museums across the country. We are particularly fortunate in living near the Newark (New Jersey) Museum, which not only has many valuable collections, but whose staff is always happy to be of use to persons who are interested in the arts or need help on projects connected with them.

They are also cognizant of the relationship between art and the natural world, and staged an unusual flower show where arrangers were invited to select their accessories from the Museum's collection of Oriental bronzes.

On a recent visit, two pieces of Oriental art which greatly appealed to us were a large stoneware jar from Korea and a folding Japanese screen with striking ink paintings of cocks on tan panels.

The Zen Buddhist artist eliminates color and detail and seeks to express the life essence of his subject. He achieves his goal with sweeping brush strokes of black ink, shading from dark to light.

It was a real challenge to find the right plant materials. They had to be related to the painted panels in design and concept and also be large and dramatic enough to use in an arrangement which would complement the screen but not be overpowered by it. In the Korean jar we placed tan, jointed, bamboolike stalks of seven-foot Heracleum, two huge seed heads and one enormous leaf from the same plant, with two unusually curved branches of Ailanthus.

126

Screen—Japan. Ink on paper by Ito Jacuchu (A.D. 1716-
1800), famous painter of roosters.

Jar—Korea. Glazed stoneware. Yi dynasty, about 17th century. Both from the collection of the Newark Museum,
N. J.; Curator of Oriental Art, Eleanor Olson.

Photographed in the Newark Museum.

127

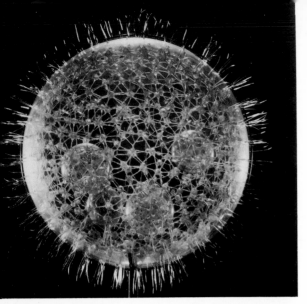

Volvox globator, Courtesy of the American Museum of Natural History.

Tubularia harrimani, Courtesy of the American Museum of Natural History.

Dorcadospyris dinoceras, Courtesy of the American Museum of Natural History.

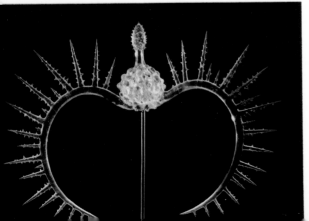

VISITS need not be limited to "art" museums. Great opportunities for study and enjoyment are offered by others, such as New York City's American Museum of Natural History.

One of its most astonishing exhibits appears in the Hall of Ocean Life. It shows what appear to be magnificent, intricately fashioned crystal jewels. In actuality these are microscopic protozoa, enlarged hundreds of times. A master glass blower devotes six months or more to each creation, and we were awestruck by the craftsmanship involved in making these models, which show us an unknown world of animals hundreds of millions of years old.

We were amazed at the fantastic construction in this "simplest form of animal life," and at nature's repetitions of forms, from an infinitesimal creature to a huge flower. But our wonder at the likenesses throughout nature only serves to emphasize the fact that no two forms are exactly alike. The greatest wonder always remains the unbelievable diversity which arises from what scientific investigation has shown to be an underlying identity of physical substance.

WALKING through the halls of a museum, we feel our great privilege in having access to these treasures of the world, examples selected and displayed by experts to show the ever-changing aspects of beauty in man's long history of creativity.

There is also the thrill of the unexpected—an exciting, recent acquisition, or the exhibit on loan from a foreign country or private collection not usually available to the general public. We will never forget the day we went to the Metropolitan Museum of Art in New York City, to do some research, and came upon "Four Hundred Winters . . . Four Hundred Springs," a display of 250 Japanese robes covering a period of 400 years.

Some of the unbelievably sumptuous, richly decorated kimonos were shown folded over garment racks against specially constructed gold-leaf screens which covered the walls from floor to ceiling. Others were draped upon wire forms, so the robes appeared to be taking part in a temple ceremony, a tea party, or a well attended stage presentation.

The design on each single robe could have been studied for hours, so varied were the methods of decoration and so wide the range of color and subject matter. This included not only flowers and birds, but fish, beasts, landscapes, cities, flower bowls, fans, flutes, books, and calligraphy. Naturally we were most interested to recognize familiar plant forms in an endless variety of embroidery stitches: appliqué, stencil dyeing, and intricate patterns of tie-and-dye, sometimes enhanced by freehand painting.

Our favorite robe showed wisteria vines and flowers. Since we wanted to have something to remind us of the display—something we could use in our own home—we made a small, dull-gold table screen, decorating it with actual wisteria branches, dried tendrils, and pressed leaves. Real wisteria blossoms are not practical for such a use, but we remembered the shell-like appearance of the three-dimensional embroidered florets. Looking over our collection of shells, we found that the small lavender coquinas in graduated sizes would make comparable wisteria racemes.

Since the screen was planned to be used as a background for a small arrangement, the vines were carried across three panels only, leaving the fourth plain. Against this are placed a few delicate branches of shell-like Pinkster azalea.

132

Croome Court Tapestry Room, gift of the Samuel H. Kress Foundation, 1958-1959; courtesy the Metropolitan Museum of Art.

As WE STEPPED into the Croome Court Tapestry Room at the Metropolitan, we found ourselves surrounded by intense pink—on walls, carpet, and furniture—with a super-abundance of embellishment. Although almost overwhelmed by the entire room we found separate motifs most appealing: the festoons of flowers, the elaborate compositions in the corners, the urn of flowers over the mantel, and the bouquets on the furniture. The flowers shown included peonies, vines, and many types of full-blown roses—all of which were blooming in our June garden.

Our variation on a Croome Court theme does not bear too great a resemblance to its inspiration, being related to its least obvious beauties. We reversed the color scheme, putting the emphasis on the flowers instead of on the background. Instead of the intense pink, our background color repeated the small amount of aqua in the room, while its pattern derives from the restrained Adam woodwork and ceiling rather than the florid Gobelin tapestry.

Instead of duplicating the bulging shape of the ormolu urn, we selected a more slender glass vase with a medallion and gilt decorations, suggested by the shape and color of the gilt furniture. A variety of forms — roses, clematis, viburnum, ferns, ivy geraniums, and passion vine—repeats the feeling of opulence.

Since the predominant color of the flowers in the tapestry was a muted yellow, we used this as the subordinate color, featuring the strong pinks.

Sometimes a museum visit may give us cause to re-evaluate our own possessions. This 17th-century Italian gate immediately called to mind a pair of long-forgotten iron wall hooks, and suggested how we could use them effectively.

By attaching two small black bottles to the hooks, we made them into containers to hold our favorite vine. And what flower arranger could fail to associate the curving and recurving designs in the gate with the like design in wisteria tendrils?

Around the containers circle stark branches in rhythmic curves. Sprays of black seed heads from the rice-paper plant (*Fatsia papyrifera*) relieve the severity of the composition while suggesting the intricate details in the gate.

Courtesy of the
Metropolitan Museum of Art;
Rogers Fund, 1905.

Pride of Possession

MUSEUMS OFFER A MULTITUDE OF IDEAS which can be applied in the pursuance of our own specialties. But they do not provide the material objects with which to realize these ideas. For them we must look to other sources, mainly among our own possessions, which we have a tendency to overlook because familiarity often dulls perception.

In museums we look at the exhibits with a vision unclouded by everyday associations. Returning home, our eyes should retain the ability to see clearly—beyond the everyday association of familiar objects to their intrinsic design. We should learn to take a fresh look at our own possessions and take pride in the beauties they have, even though they may not qualify as museum pieces.

In this way we have rediscovered the charm of many things—including an old metal wall bracket which the children had used as a catchall for school souvenirs. We knew nothing about its origin, had never before actually "seen" it, completely overlooking the loveliness of its openwork pattern of delicate ribbonlike festoons.

We painted it white and used it as a container for flowers. This decoration became a feature in the sunroom. In the two holders andromeda, hyacinths, and narcissus are arranged in casual but compact bouquets. Sprays of small-leaved ivy frame the bracket and repeat the gentle curves of the metal drapery.

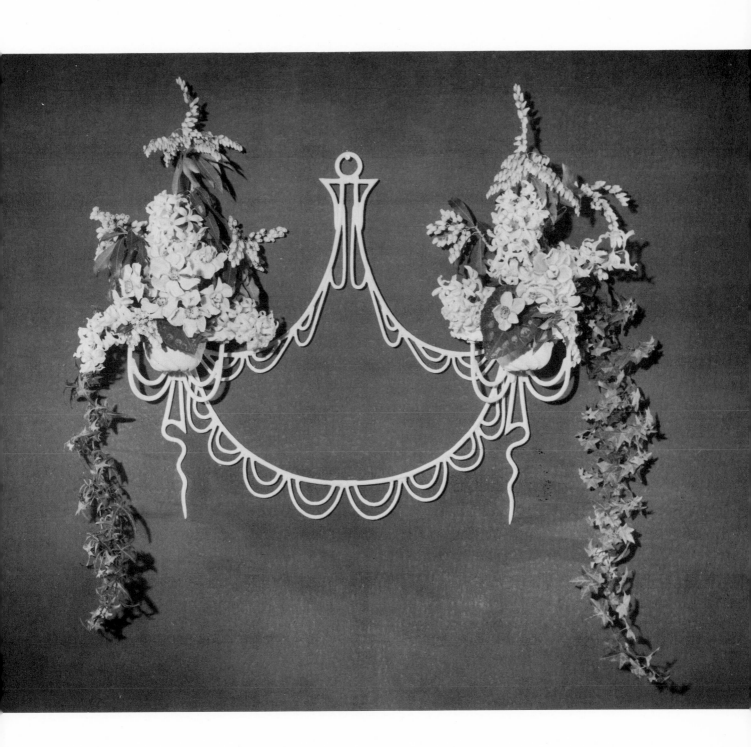

SOMETIMES ONE IS FORTUNATE enough to own a treasure so precious that familiarity merely increases its appeal. Such a one is this carved wood angel. In addition to the beauty of form and the pleasing patina of age, there is that expressiveness which makes an object even more beautiful by suggestion.

Santayana says, "What constitutes the individual expressiveness of things is the circle of thoughts allied to each in a given mind," and the angel is a vivid symbol of those things which have a power over the Christian mind. All of those things become a part of the imaginative value of this ideal object. It evokes, consciously or unconsciously, memories of the masterpieces of Christian art through the centuries; great cathedrals and the hundreds of nameless craftsmen who built and decorated them; the grandeur of the church service, star-tipped tapers, the peal of the organ, and swelling choruses of praise.

From this background we choose settings for the angel, sometimes placing it beside a towering candle, sometimes below an ancient page of music, accompanied by intertwining leaves like a border of illuminated manuscript.

But the closest association is with the Virgin Mary, to whom the angel said, "Hail, thou that art highly favored . . . blessed art thou among women . . . And behold, thou shalt . . . bring forth a son, and shalt call his name Jesus . . . and of his kingdom there shall be no end." And the symbol of Mary is the lily.

THE CARVED ANGEL would lend itself to use in many settings, but there are other things which are more demanding in their requirements of color, style, and design in accompanying arrangements. Such a piece is any silhouette picture, where the immediate impression comes from the clean-cut outlines of stark black against white. Equally clean-cut outlines of dark against light must be carried out in the plant material, containers, and accessories.

This particular 18th-century painting on glass has, in addition, an unusual amount of detail: delicate furniture, urns on pedestals, and a festoon motif in the drapery and in the ornamentation on the table. Although the scene is an informal family gathering, there is a definite formality throughout, due partly to the period depicted and partly to the symmetrically balanced placement of the individual subjects.

Selection and arrangement of all elements of composition must reflect these different aspects. Symmetrical, rather two-dimensional designs are made in bronze urns with festoon decoration. Round white straw flowers are surrounded by green and white geranium leaves against a background of near-black, glycerined Pyracantha and blueberry foliage, which is silhouetted against the white wall.

The square black bases under the containers repeat the angles and the solidity of the picture frame, while the lids of the urns repeat the curve of the chair backs and complete the circle of interest.

141

142

NOT EVERYONE POSSESSES ART OBJECTS which are of outstanding interest, but almost all of us have a good many undistinguished things which are treasured mainly for their sentimental associations. This Paisley shawl, the needlepoint bellpull, oval flower paintings, black-and-gold fan, and ruby glass lustres fall into this category.

Since they are all Victorian we combine them with plant material which is Victorian in design and color, but arrange it in a manner that reflects the current desire for clearly defined outlines. Large bright flowers—full-blown coral-colored roses, frilly red Coleus, and royal purple Buddleia—are the dominant feature, in contrast to the many muted, small patterns in the various accessories.

By bringing together several of these "family pieces" and adding plant material, we have created a nostalgic grouping which achieves as a whole a distinction not found in any one single part.

THE POSSESSION of any number of family pieces does not keep one from looking at new and different things with an acquisitive eye. We are all confirmed collectors, and become even more so with the discovery of subjects related to our special interests.

Naturally the flower arranger collects unusual plant material, containers, and accessories—each one according to her own tastes. We ourselves find the greatest joy and inspiration in Oriental art, since, of all the world's art, this is most closely allied to the natural world. The Oriental regards nature with a deep feeling of appreciation as the common source from which all life comes. To him the meaning of life and art is found in this appreciation.

The unusual figures shown here are the work of some perceptive Oriental artist to whom the shapes of two gnarled roots had suggested the contours of a proud lady and a humble peasant. With a minimum of masterful carving he brought out the characters which he had envisioned in the wood.

An obvious setting for these root carvings would be a gnarled branch such as is seen in Oriental paintings, but this would be an association too close in all areas of reference, resulting in a loss of emphasis for the figures. Instead they were given their due importance by combining them with material contrasting in type although related in substance and texture.

We selected strong, sculptured forms with interesting texture, variety in shape and size, and contrast in lights and darks: woody palm spathes, large, thick leaves of sea-grape (*Coccolobis uvifera*), tall gracefully curving branches of bottle-brush (*Melaleuca*) on which are clustered the woody seed cases—and three "carved" fish-poison pods (*Barringtonia speciosa*).

Burl bases raised the figures to different levels and added needed visual weight to the accessory grouping. A grass mat hung at the right is a light, textured background for the dark carvings, and repeats the color of the sea-grape and bottle-brush leaves. A mat of heavier texture is used as a base for the naturalistic cedar bowl.

This composition combines pieces from an art collection and a plant-material collection. Both were built up item by item from various parts of the world—providing pleasure in the seeking, the finding, and the using.

As WE HAVE SAID, any art object can be greatly enhanced by the addition of complementary plant material, but it is not always desirable that this plant material be the dominant feature. In a composition where objects of outstanding interest are used, it is often better that the plant material assume the subordinate role.

This certainly applies to the use of such a treasure as the Chinese bronze wine vessel shown here. It was patterned after a prototype of the Shang dynasty (1500-1000 B.C.), but made during the Sung dynasty (960-1279 A.D.) when collectors were just beginning to seek—and have copied—those astonishing archaic bronzes which have no counterpart anywhere in the world.

But the history of this piece was not the governing factor in our choice of accompanying plant material. Instead, material was chosen because it was of comparable visual quality—harmonious in color, texture, and substance. An Oriental carved stand holds an accessory arrangement of citron, Cycas pods, Ochrosia fruits, and a cluster of Carissa fruits and foliage.

A small, standing bronze figure behind the fruit contributes depth and balance to the composition. The large, proportionately varied areas of space within the design unify its three distinct features, while emphasizing the importance of each.

After having completed this composition, we recalled that the sweet-smelling citron is a favorite fruit of the Chinese, and is called "Buddha's hand" fruit. This was a bit of unintentional association which we found enchanting. We add another:

"We sacrifice with pure wine . . .
The fruit offering follows . . .
So strong-smelling, so sweet smelling,
So hallowed, so shining an offering
To august ancestors,
Who reward us with blessings,
With long life never ending."

The Book of Songs
(Chou Dynasty, 1112-249 B.C.)
Edited by Robert Payne

146

147

IN WORKING toward a finished composition, it really doesn't matter from which point one starts. Inspiration can be drawn from a container, plant material, or an abstract idea. The main consideration is the final harmony of all elements. This arrangement was not inspired by the fine bronze container, not by the interesting branches of *Euonymus alatus*, but by a page of Japanese calligraphy. We could not translate these word characters into our language of words, but we could translate the abstract brushwork design into the design language of the natural world.

To match the strong silhouette of the characters, material would almost have to be found in bare branches. We studied many trees and shrubs, asking ourselves which strong, dark stems grow in an angular fashion with both short and long, sweeping curves. Some of the hawthorne trees or shrubs appeared at first to have possibilities. However, their thorns were too regularly spaced and even in length for the irregular pattern of the calligraphy. The long branches of the winged elm lacked the angularity in design we were searching for. But the winged Euonymus met all the requirements, with a few extra "brush strokes" added.

Only then was the tall bronze vase chosen for its style, weight, and silhouette—the sharp detail of its outline which resembles the formation of the winged Euonymus. Two twiggy branches, when pruned slightly and set in the container, became a natural calligraphy design.

窂觀波、唐云高顯、亦曰方墳、或安寧軆、或安舍

圖塔也、古譯或藐偸覈、或曰塔婆、誐言

皆訛略不正、窂觀波正梵云偸覈也、下經文云以三

焦上金剛界分智威力加持、頌證毗盧遮那之身

流出無量佛頂法身、於□集空中、以成法會光明

護法界、展轉出□□□□、如來毗盧遮那

輪、十地滿足□□□波、階級衛護

應知現證、本有三身、流出塵刹、無屬聚集

維亦名窂都波郎、足毗盧遮那金身、深可熟察

菩薩金剛

Detail of the lacquer work
on the cabinet.

AN ARRANGEMENT used in a home setting is part of the over-all scheme of decoration. Its style, color, and size must be considered in relation to its placement in the room and to the appointments with which it is used. Art objects such as this highly decorated lacquer cabinet and long, narrow Chinese clock usually set the keynote for a whole room. The rich ornamentation of the cabinet dictated the type of accessories used with it: Oriental, elegant, opulent—golden.

Rather than duplicate the actual material seen in the painted design, we use forms which will provide variety in line, texture, and dimension, even when they are all gilded. Dried Boston fern, Echinops, pokeweed, and long-fingered leaves of *Jatropha texana* set the design. Dried magnolia leaves and dogwood blossoms provide transition. Cedar cones add weight and sculptured forms at the edge of the Chinese brass container.

152

ALTHOUGH THE ART OF THE FAR EAST is dear to every flower arranger, other arts and crafts also have appeal and are equally challenging to the imagination. One of the earliest crafts—one more closely associated with the Western world—is glassmaking, the oldest known pure glass being a molded Egyptian amulet of about 7000 B.C. From 1550 B.C. to the Christian era, Egypt was the center of the glass industry, but the golden age of glass was the first four centuries, when Roman glassmakers were producing colored vases of such beauty that they were more precious than gold or silver.

Venetian glass dates back to the 11th century, but it was in the 16th century that the Venetians found the way to express the true Renaissance sense of form in spirited, graceful, airy shapes springing entirely from the glassblower's techniques. Death penalties were imposed upon glassworkers taking the secret of their process abroad, but in spite of this the method spread throughout Europe where individual styles were developed.

Venetian glass in the main has remained loyal to its typical shapes, but in the last few years certain artists have ventured into new fields, creating smooth glass "sculpture," such as our colorful pigeon.

Scandinavian glassmaking is a comparatively recent development but in a remarkably short time has taken a prominent place in the field. The Venetian bird and Swedish bowl, though from widely separated countries and traditions, belong together. Their simplicity, smooth lines, and glowing colors are reflected in the arrangement.

153

Fused glass by Dorothy Larson. Shelf and mirror mounting by Martin Stan Buchner.

154

Craftsmen's Associations

CHINESE BRONZES AND VENETIAN GLASS — we seemed to have traveled a long way from our first visit to a Maine craft shop. We suddenly realized that we had been losing sight of the work being done now in our own country. In a way this is more important than anything else, for on the public's interest in our crafts of today rests the existence of tomorrow's crafts — with all their value for the individual and the community.

Remembering the Maine Coast Craftsmen, we looked for such an organization in our own state and found the New Jersey Designer-Craftsmen, who had come together ten years before for the purpose of exchanging ideas and bringing their work to the attention of the public. Up until this time there had been no exhibitions in the state to show the work of professional craftsmen, but today juried shows are held each year to which anyone may submit work. When the American Craftsmen's Council was formed, the New Jersey group joined it, to work with groups all across the country in what may well prove to be a real Renaissance in crafts.

Our introduction to the New Jersey Designer-Craftsmen came through an exhibit staged in the little town of Hanover, in the showrooms of one of its members, Martin Stan Buchner, designer of custom-made furniture. Among the various pieces shown were a matching mirror and table shelf. The fused-glass panels and tile are the work of one member of the group, set into a frame and a shelf made by another member.

The mirror decoration was made up of a series of rectangular panels. Within each panel many small pieces of glass were fused together with an overlay pattern of bent wires and wire mesh. The colors were muted orange, yellow, amber, and green. The mirror and shelf, hanging on a pale yellow wall, made an ideal showcase for a simple line arrangement of bittersweet and Freesias.

A mirror dramatizes whatever it reflects in its duplication of line and form; but this duplication must be considered as part of the design of any composition placed before it — as was done here. The massed flowers are not quite doubled, but two branches of bittersweet in silhouette seem to be four branches.

The overlapping planes of the glass bottle, its partial shadow and reflection create an impression of depth and are a repetition of the angular pattern in the frame and shelf.

156

Bench by Michael Galardi.
Rug by Norma Fox.
Planter by Martin Stan Buchner.
Ceramics by Edward Chandless.

THE EXHIBITION of the New Jersey Designer-Craftsmen included work of many types, not only furniture and glass, but jewelry, other metal and enamel work, weaving, and ceramics, all showing the qualities which come only from meticulous handwork, and all following the modern style but in various ways.

In a home grouping we noted the satin finish of the furniture with its unembellished simplicity, the texture of the striped, woven rug, and the matt glaze of the ceramics with their decorated surfaces — each craft complementing the other.

One piece which naturally appealed to us was a long, low planter of polished wood and Fiberglas. It enabled us to make a composition of living plants, carrying out the variations in design seen in the furniture and accessories. Counterparts were found in the papyrus with its simplicity and freedom of line, the striped spider plant, and the broad leaves of variegated arrowhead (*Nephthytis*) with its decorated leaf surfaces.

The plants are placed to create strong silhouettes, a variety of levels, and well proportioned areas of space which dramatize each individual grouping. They introduce two vertical patterns in contrast to the predominantly horizontal lines of the furniture.

Earthenware fish by Edward Chandless, partly wheel thrown and partly hand built, decorated in a wax-resist and sgraffito technique.

Woven hanging
by Norma Fox.

ANOTHER ITEM seen at the New Jersey Designer-Craftsmen exhibit was this unusual open-weave hanging, which makes a most versatile room divider. It was fascinating to discover how light from one direction brought out the interesting diagonal weft pattern, while light from another direction caught the vertical warp threads and created a three-dimensional effect.

It is also an excellent setting for a plant or arrangement which can be seen to advantage from either side of the hanging. For maximum effect, any plant material used should give the same feeling of openness and should have strong linear design and silhouette value. Heracleum has these qualities. Two branching stalks and seed heads seem to weave another pattern across the gauzy fabric.

158

OF ALL THE CONTACTS we have made with craftsmen, perhaps the most deeply moving have been those with two musicians — the violinmaker Alvah M. Batchelder of Frankfort, Maine, U.S.A., and the flute maker Ziphion Azta of Tel Aviv, Israel. One of these men is old, one is young. They come from widely separated countries and traditions. Yet both are afire with the same joy of creation, the same intense dedication of the music maker.

Many violinists feel that Batchelder violins are unsurpassed in our age, and they are being played in nearly every major orchestra in the country. He has repaired violins of all the great makers of history: not only Stradivari, Amati, and Guarneri, but Viullaume, Mittenwohl, Klotz, Stainer, Pamphilon. "I can compare the workmanship — and it's the workmanship — that makes it a fiddle or a master violin," said Mr. Batchelder when we visited him.

He had made his first violin at the age of 19 and, at the age of 82, was making number 88. He was working on the back, a beautiful piece of Maine curly maple, perfectly graduated from 6/64 inch at the edge to 12/64 inch at the center (graduations vary according to the texture of each individual piece of wood) and smoothly finished inside as well as out, so no roughness would break the sound vibrations.

"When I was young," he told us, "it was the excitement of wondering how it would turn out. Now I know it will have a good tone. It's the pleasure of making it. But of course one can be better than another. When I make the next violin exactly like the last because I think I've got it perfected, then I'll quit. I don't foresee that time."

Mr. Batchelder is a retired blacksmith, and makes his own tools for violinmaking. He is following in the footsteps of his father who was also the village blacksmith as well as violinmaker and popular dance fiddler. But today in the United States this kind of craftsmanship is vanishing. There is no young apprentice to whom Alvah Batchelder can pass on the craft which he has pursued with such skill and joy. "If there were only someone to whom I could leave the knowledge I have gained," he said to us, a deep sadness momentarily dimming his vitality and enthusiasm.

ZIPHION AZTA is both musician and dancer with Inbal, the dance theater of Israel. He and his fellow members are all fired with the consciousness that they are part of a group and a nation which are striving to create a fresh and living tradition. They find no sadness in the thought of the future to dim their passionate dedication.

Their new idioms in music and dance spring from age-old roots, and they guard carefully the life-giving sources — their religious faith and their ancient culture in all its phases. Costumes and jewelry are authentic. They are made by an organization which preserves the ancient skills brought to Israel by the Oriental and North African immigrants. Material is handwoven, with 40 different kinds of threads and weaves.

For the major new work, "Desert," Oriental-Arabic melodies were gathered from the members of Inbal, who are of Oriental origin — mainly Yemenite — and arranged by Sara Levi-Tanai, director and founder of Inbal. The music is played on specially constructed Oriental instruments, including the Chang, the Shofar, and the Arab flutes made by Mr. Azta. In "Desert" he uses ten different bamboo flutes, in alto, tenor, and soprano. These are modeled after the Arabic flutes, but with eight finger holes instead of the original four or five which would not play the chromatic scale.

Of all the dances of Inbal, we found "Desert" the most compelling. It is "an Oriental creation, but universal in its very depths, depicting the passions and confusions that beset man because he is man." The sequences include: Ancient Song . . . Caravan . . . Oases . . . He and She . . . Clouds of Sand . . . Mirage . . . and Whereto? The notes of the flute, in ascending spirals, express the longing of man for the oases of beauty and love, as his caravan moves, in its eternal trail, across the symbolic desert.

A. M. Balchelder. No. 88 Frankfort, Me. 1960

UNLIKE the interpretation which we made for "Desert," the violin arrangement was done without reference to association with period or locality. An elegant 18th-century arrangement would have reflected the times of Stradivari, while an arrangement of field flowers would have brought to mind the old-fashioned hoe-down and dance fiddler.

But we thought of Mr. Batchelder, and the look in his eyes as he held up a violin against the light of the window and asked, "Did you ever see anything more beautiful than those curves? Did you ever see anything more beautiful than a violin?"

So we chose as our inspiration the abstract designs seen in the instrument itself and the rhythm of the notes through which it fulfills its ultimate purpose. Each branch of wisteria and akebia vine, with leaf notes and spiraling tendrils, was selected for its relationship to the design and music of the beautiful violin.

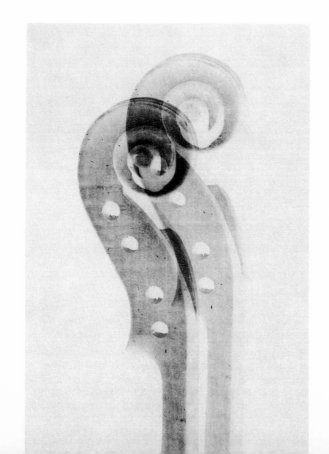

PART **IV**

Flower Show

Work in the healthful and relaxing atmosphere of a greenhouse is of great benefit to the mentally disturbed.

A patient of the greenhouse detail at Lyons Veterans' Hospital collects lupine pods for use in dried arrangements during the winter.

In this prize-winning arrangement made by a patient, there is close textural relationship between the plaque made in the Ceramics Department and plant material from the Garden Therapy Department.

Veterans' Hospital

THE ORIENTALS have long realized the therapeutic value of observing and working with nature — how anger and unhappiness fade as one patiently trims and trains a bonsai tree. Now, in the West, it is understood that losing oneself in any absorbing, creative work is of the greatest value to the whole human being.

With normal people this sense of well-being is merely an extra dividend derived from work which is mainly designed to be productive. But when arts and crafts are considered as therapy, to aid the physical and/or mentally disabled in the achievement of psychological, social, and economic restoration, the result to be evaluated is not so much the tangible product as the intangible benefit derived from the work by the patient.

Painting, music, crafts, and greenhouse and horticultural activities are used as specialized therapies in hospitals and institutions across the country. The paid staffs are supplemented by volunteer organizations. Garden club members aid in carrying out the horticultural programs. At the request of the authorities of Lyons Veterans' Hospital, where all the patients are under psychiatric treatment, the Garden Club of New Jersey formed the Green Thumb Corps wherein each volunteer from a local club gives at least 100 hours a year in garden-therapy activities. We feel it a great privilege to be a part of this group.

Members are on a regular schedule and work with the patients throughout the continuing cycle of

Materials from both the Garden Therapy and the Craft Department are combined in this 8-foot decorated panel, the keynote at the 1959 Flower Show, "Festival of Flowers and Crafts."

the seasons, from the first seed planting in the greenhouse, through transplanting, propagating, weeding, pruning, and finally cutting and arranging of the flowers for use in the hospital. These add a note of brightness to the wards, the libraries, and the reception rooms. A large percentage of the Christmas decorations are also made at the greenhouse.

At the same time, our organization provides the patients with a healthful association with the community that cannot be furnished by the paid staff regardless of its size and effectiveness. We make it possible for the greenhouse group of patients to attend many local flower shows and even to exhibit in competition with the general public.

From this participation, interest was generated among the patients for a flower show of their own. The first show, in 1951, was held in a small room since there were only 50 entries. The last show was held in the large auditorium with more than 300 entries, and the V. A. Garden Club of Lyons is now a fully accredited member of the Garden Club of New Jersey.

The show is supervised by the Physical Medicine and Rehabilitation Service of the hospital. The

Details of the "wind chime" show the use of plant material grown in the hospital gardens with shells brought in by the Green Thumb volunteers.

Crown of thorns and Echeveria grown in the hospital greenhouse and a Nubian head on a bamboo raft are selected by a patient to make an exotic composition.

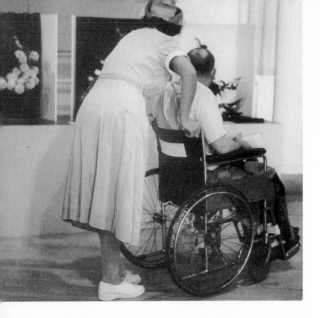

Physically handicapped patients are brought to the Flower Show with the help of volunteer workers.

patients are directly involved in the planning, mechanics, and exhibiting. The competitive classes are also open to the public; this means that the patients compete not only with one another, but with staff members and experienced flower arrangers from garden clubs all over the state.

Horticultural specimens which have been cared for by the men during the growing season are carefully groomed for the show, and are also in competition with specimens grown by the public. Awards are made by qualified judges, as in any standard show. Local commercial, professional, and educational organizations present many displays to enhance the show, which draws more than 500 visitors from the surrounding communities.

In a recent show the entire schedule was based on the interrelationship between crafts and plant material. It was called "The Festival of Flowers and Crafts." Each class called for an arrangement to include a material or a project from the craft activities of the hospital: leatherwork, metalwork, weaving, woodcraft, or ceramics.

In the spring when the schedule was written, the patients in the craft classes were acquainted with the type of show to be held in September. Their projects were planned with the show in mind, which provided a very definite incentive. Samples of this work were shown to the men in the greenhouse therapy department. With the help of the Green Thumb Corps, they worked out their plans for arrangements to go with the crafts.

There is usually one large exhibit which carries out the general theme of the show and is a featured attraction. This is one of the long-term projects and

Men often stand for long periods of time, taking in every detail in one of the exhibits.

Patients, families, friends, and general public all attend the show.

A gigantic "wind chime" was made in the Garden Therapy greenhouse.

is carried out over many weeks. For this particular show an entire 4' x 8' sheet of plywood was used as a background for a flower and craft plaque. This included plant material collected and dried by the men in the greenhouse group throughout the summer, metal and ceramic objects made by patients in the craft department, and materials used in the crafts, such as leather and rug yarn. It was constructed by patients and Green Thumb Corps members, who worked at it for approximately six weeks during August and September.

Another large exhibit, which occupied more workers over an even longer period of time, was an enormous "wind chime" made of over 40 pieces of translucent plastic cut in various shapes and sizes. Each one was painted with a design, or decorated with dried plant material and shells which were glued on both sides of the plastic so the pattern would be attractive as these "mobiles" turned. The shells were brought in by the volunteers, but most of the plant material came from the hospital gardens.

All the patients who are able take part in the show in some way. Some help in setting it up, some act as guides, some compete, and others merely enjoy the beauty, the novelty, and the contact with the public. Patients from other psychiatric hospitals also attend the show.

No one knows from what one facet a patient derives benefit, but we do know that this therapy in its many aspects helps the men in the difficult transition from institutional life to life in the outside world. To have worked with a patient who had not spoken to anyone for months, and then gradually had achieved communication — seeing the barriers dissolve through association with growing plants and sympathetic people — is an extraordinary and gratifying experience. The first time we heard the patient speak, and finally the day he was ready to leave — going off with his family to start life again — these were days to remember.

The metalliclike Echeveria in a patient's blue ribbon composition reflects the pink-copper sheen of hand-wrought candlesticks and tray.

Materials of the Craft

"FESTIVAL OF FLOWERS AND CRAFTS" would make a good theme for any flower show. Flower arrangers have always used the work of craftsmen, and craftsmen have always been inspired by nature, but a flower show whose theme was deliberately planned to illuminate the underlying meaning of both arts and their relationship to each other would be of great importance and interest.

In one section educational features would be incorporated within each composition, resulting in exhibits which would not only be beautiful but have a greater breadth of interest than usual. This would also be a judicious use of space, which is often at a premium in standard shows where a specified number of sections must be included.

The first idea that comes to mind for such a section in a show of this type is:

Materials of the Crafts — Educational and Arrangement Section

> In the following classes the working materials used in a particular craft must be included. The finished product may also be used as either container or accessory. Some fresh plant material is required.

CLASS 1. *Block Printing*

> From our trip to Maine we remember the work of Stell and Shevis, and realize that we could make an unusual flower-show exhibit from the various aspects of their craft: the carved blocks, proofs made from them, and the plant material of which their designs reminded us.
>
> One block had shown a large snowflake pattern suggested by the radiating design of wild parsnip. A similar pattern appeared in a block print featuring Siamese cats with big round staring eyes like the black-eyed susans in the fields all around us. The educational part of the composition could include carving tools, ink, the roller used to spread it on the blocks, and the series of wood blocks for the two-color prints of a calendar on which short grass heads were glued, taking the place of man-made carving.

173

CLASS 2. *Woodcraft*

OF all the materials with which man can work, wood is one of the most satisfying. It is pleasing to the touch, the sight, and the smell, and holds within itself infinite possibilities for the creation of objects of great beauty. One flowingly grained bowl, carved in the shape of a Calla-lily leaf and highly polished, naturally suggested the use of Calla lilies and their leaves.

To conform to the section title, "Materials of the Craft," we include other types of wood: a large unfinished maple burl as a base; a plank of Hawaiian wood, partially finished and partly unfinished, behind the arrangement; a carved board against a pattern of overlapping rectangles of variously grained wood samples. Some of these are white and velvety like the Calla lilies. The dull, rough-textured background of coco matting emphasizes the shapes and high polish of the various wood pieces.

175

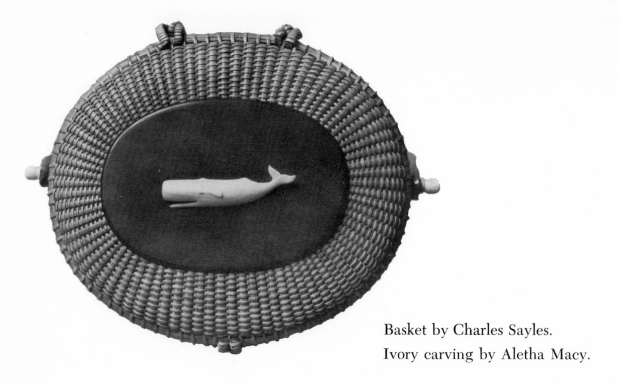

Basket by Charles Sayles.

Ivory carving by Aletha Macy.

CLASS 3. *A Craft Indigenous to One Geographical Area*

THERE is a modern craft indigenous to a particular area which gives its name to the product — the Nantucket basket. This finely woven basket is topped with an ebony plaque on which a genial ivory whale tosses a flippant tail. It is a combination of two traditional crafts of early New England, basketry and scrimshaw, the ivory carving done by sailors on the old sailing vessels.

Today this is no longer done by unnamed craftsmen whiling away the long hours at sea, but by two women who are consciously keeping alive a tradition which would otherwise be lost in our madly racing civilization which whiles away its leisure hours in very different pursuits.

For our exhibit we feature the atmosphere of Nantucket, setting up a corner of an imaginary workshop. The completed basket is shown with a bundle of reed, slices and sections of ivory tusk, the tools used in carving them, ivory beads and an intricately carved ivory box which could have been brought from distant ports by one of the sea captains of whaling days. Work such as this no doubt inspired the sailors in their own unique scrimshaw.

At the right, heather, which covers the rolling meadows of the island, is combined with weathered driftwood and cork floats from the shore. Through the latticed window we catch a glimpse of drying nets and a lone sea gull.

Museum Exhibit

CLASS 1.   *Design in Nature.*

An integrated composition of natural forms treated as individual art objects. Fresh and/or dried plant material must predominate. Photographs of natural forms may be included. A list of plant material and its origin must accompany the exhibit.

THE number of forms which would qualify as natural works of art is overwhelming. The problem is to select specimens which will have an intrinsic design of great interest with variety in texture, size, shape, and substance, and yet will combine to make a harmonious over-all composition.

Our starting point was a so-called "Encino arbol crest," which is a strange growth formed at the top of the live oak — an explosion of the wood's cells caused by the action of a clinging parasite plant similar to the mistletoe. This distortion of nature is so fantastic that in Mexico it is believed by the superstitious to have supernatural powers.

The new growth of the palmetto had also been distorted, not by nature, but by man when he bulldozed the land where it grew. The normal growth of papyrus, with its radiating leaf segments, tall cranelike Schefflera stems, curving banana stalk, fruit and flower, and a digger pine cone with its distinct, measured pattern, provide extremes of contrast in structure.

Stones, sculptured by nature, make an accessory grouping. Two of these are dramatized in an enlarged photograph, as are the details of the "carved" banana stem and the pleated palmetto.

The elements of the composition are arranged in two main groupings which are unified by direction of plant material and by placement of the largest photograph.

178

179

CLASS 2.   *Far Countries.*

A scene to interpret the essential charactertistics of any far country. Fresh plant material must predominate but need not be indigenous to the area. Artifacts from the country must be used.

FOR our "far country" we chose Africa, although—or perhaps because —we had never visited it. There is a fascination about the unknown, or rather the partially known, where one has just enough information to spark the imagination.

We assembled three African artifacts: a totem pole, an idol, and a boatlike container in the shape of a crocodile. These represented magic, religion, and tribal life, basic elements of primitive existence. In spite of much reading, we still did not know the real meaning of these symbols, and could only strive to create about them the atmosphere of mystery, lush tropical growth, and violent color which, it seemed to us, represented so much of the dark continent.

In the crocodile boat we placed a tall arrangement with unusual outline of forms and startling contrasts of color, the interrupted rhythms suggesting the movements of an African dance. Colors run from scarlet through magenta and intense purple, with touches of yellow, copper, green, chartreuse, brown, and black.

Although the material is not all from Africa, with the exception of the magenta-and-coral *Magnolia tripetala* seed pods, it is all from the tropics: cockscomb, passion flower, Melastoma, zinnias, Cannas, Peperomia, coconut, and the spearlike black pods of the "African Tulip Tree" (*Spathodea Africana*).

These pods are also used as a spear motif with the ceremonial grouping at the back. Although the ritual objects are small, they are given due importance by their position. The arrangement frames them on one side, and the Schefflera "trees" and a pineapple plant frame them on the other. A red glow on the background behind the idol further dramatizes them and adds mystery to the jungle scene.

180

CLASS 3. *Form and Space.*

A collection of natural and man-made forms demonstrating the use of space within a given area. All objects to be from one particular craft. Some fresh plant material must be included.

O̲UR first idea was to show the progression of styles of glass from old ornate pieces to smooth modern ones, with comparable plant material. We gathered together examples of old and new glass in many types and colors. Such a collection was interesting in theory, but when we put it together we discovered that there were many discordant notes. We eliminated one ornate piece after another — ending with both old and new, but all related through simplicity of design.

To fill all areas of space within the niche to best advantage, we first suspended a glass shelf at the upper left. This held a large, old glass jar containing two dried allium seed heads, and two old bottles, one of which held curving sprays of variegated honeysuckle (*Lonicera japonica aureo-reticulata*).

A modern frosted-glass bowl holding fresh allium flowers and variegated Hosta leaves was placed at the lower right on two glass bases. These two diagonally opposite areas established a framework for the composition. An old covered bowl and two modern frosted-glass birds on two levels at low center carry the eye from one group to the other.

The two remaining open areas at top right and lower left were further divided by suspended stars. Two dark-violet bottles used as a single unit at the left help balance the strong visual weight of the purple flowers at the right.

Fused-glass stars by Priscilla Porter.

184

Fused-glass bird by Priscilla Porter.

Glass

The following classes must include glass in some form. Fresh plant material is to be used exclusively. Each composition is to be given a title by the exhibitor.

CLASS 1.   *A Composition, Analogous Colors to Predominate*

PRISCILLA PORTER'S GLASS STARS were so distinctive that we looked for more of her work and discovered a fabulous bird which glowed in tones of chartreuse, green and blue, filling the specifications for a class calling for a predominance of analogous colors. A glass container would seem the obvious choice, but its color would be dulled when filled with plant material. Instead we used a ceramic vase of green-blue, almost startling in its intensity. The very high glaze applied over a rough texture was an excellent equivalent to the textured shimmering glass.

The spring garden and the greenhouse provided an abundance of plant material from which to choose colors vivid enough to balance the brilliance of the bird. Chartreuse appeared in the bird in the smallest amount, therefore chartreuse bells-of-Ireland and young tulip-tree (*Liriodendron tulipfera*) foliage were featured in the arrangement.

Delphinium of deep lapis-lazuli blue repeated the predominant color in the glass while providing height. The tulip-tree branches created an outline to complement the design of the bird. Round heads of hydrangea offset the possibility of too many verticals. Their color shaded from chartreuse to blue, but was of a paler tone than that of the bells-of-Ireland and delphinium.

The suspended bird is flying into the tall spires of delphinium which curve to meet it. The rhythmic movement of the arrangement repeats the idea of "Bird in Flight," our selected title.

CLASS 2.   *A Composition or Scene, Monochromatic Color to Predominate*

THERE is great fascination in the distortion of objects seen through panes of glass with an irregular surface. Since the schedule makes no restrictions as to the form of glass to be used, we placed such a pane across our niche, dividing it in half.

We experimented with various types of plant material, noting the patterns which resulted when they were placed behind the glass. The usual leafy or flowering material lost its identity, but bold forms with unbroken outlines created a changed, but still recognizable repetition of the original shapes, like reflections in a pond when the surface is broken by ripples.

A huge Agave plant which had outgrown our greenhouse, and a sculptured Echeveria filled these requirements for bold form. They also filled the schedule's requirements for a predominantly monochromatic color scheme, since both were the same grayed blue-green.

The center of the Agave was separated, layer by layer. The smallest, palest spikes from the heart were grouped in the back half of the niche in company with a smooth glass bird. The larger outer spikes were placed in the foreground beside the Echeverias, whose two flower stalks framed the "reflection" behind the glass.

The unreal shapes of the Agave spikes, and their even less real repetition in the distance, created a landscape which might be a vision of "The Other Side of the Moon."

Will this be the shape of tomorrow, when, perhaps, our "common" treasures of the earth will have become as rare and desirable to mankind as are today the treasures of the moon? Or will there come a time when our greatest desire will be for a simple basket of wild flowers, a bowl of fruit, a sheaf of wheat, or a stalk of lilies?

189